Object Technology
Centers of Excellence

Timothy D. Korson and Vijay K. Vaishnavi

MANNING

Greenwich
(74° w. long.)

The publisher offers discounts on this book when ordered in quantity.
For more information, please contact:

Special Sales Department
Manning Publications Co.
3 Lewis Street
Greenwich, CT 06830

Fax: (203) 661-9018
email: 73150.1431@compuserve.com

Recognizing the importance of preserving what has been written, it is the policy
of Manning to have the books they publish printed on acid-free paper, and we
exert our best efforts to that end.

Library of Congress Cataloging-in-Publication Data
Korson, Tim.
    Object technology centers of excellence / Timothy Korson and
Vijay Vaishnavi.
       p.   cm.
    Includes bibliographical references and index.
    ISBN 1-884777-16-3 (alk. paper)
    1. Object-oriented programming (Computer science)
I. Vaishnavi, Vijay. II. Title.
QA76.64.K69 1996
658.4'038—dc20   95-48208
                                     CIP

 Manning Publications Co.
3 Lewis Street
Greenwich, CT 06830

Managing editor: Lee E. Fitzpatrick
Copyeditor: Barbara Ofek
Typesetter: Aaron Lyon
Cover designer: Fernando Gonzalez Bunster

Printed in the United States of America
1 2 3 4 5 6 7 8 9 10 – BB – 00 99 98 97 96

contents

2 IBM's object-oriented technology center

TOM KRISTEK, GEOFF HAMBRICK, AND TOM GUINANE

3 GSF Object Center, BNR Ltd.

GERARD MESZAROS

4 *The Travelers' Object Systems Center*

JOHN CUNNINGHAM

5 *WilTel Technology Center*

JAMIE ERBES

preface

This book has its roots in a series of OOPSLA workshops on "The Role of a Corporate Object Technology Center" starting with OOPSLA '93. There was general agreement among participants that the position papers submitted to the workshop should be developed into case studies on object technology centers. The core of the current book is a set of four contributed case studies that cover the experience gained on object technology centers at IBM, BNR, The Travelers Group, and WilTel.

The first OTC workshop at OOPSLA '93 has grown into a sequence of yearly workshops at OOPSLA and a yearly conference on object technology centers sponsored by the Consortium for the Management of Emerging Software Technologies (Comsoft). This book has been greatly influenced by these workshops, conferences, and the Comsoft OTC Newsletter. For example, the list of OTC activities which appears in some form in all the chapters was developed in the 1993 workshop, and the first survey of these activities was reported in the 1994 workshop.

This book's purpose is to provide managers and technology insertion specialists with guidance on setting up a corporate infrastructure for object technology. The OTCs discussed are representative of the diversity in OTCs which range from grassroots organizations to formal committees to funded entities. An important theme of the book is lessons learned in introducing object technology.

This book's primary audience is any individual or group participating in setting up and running the corporate infrastructure necessary for a successful transition to object technology, as well as those charged with justifying and approving such infrastructures. A secondary audience is anyone interested in the current state of object technology within corporations.

We begin with an introductory chapter providing general advice on the goals, activities, and organization of an object technology center. The next four chapters are case studies of specific OTCs which focus on the specific cultural and technical factors relevant to the featured center. The topics covered in these chapters include the following: mission, activities, evolution, and lessons learned. Another chapter presents a survey of seven OTCs which were among those whose representatives participated in the first Object Technology Centers Conference in 1995 (OTC '95). We conclude with a chapter that synthesizes the case studies and relates them back to the generic material presented in the first chapter.

This book owes its existence to the series of OTC workshops at the OOPSLA conference, and the conference on object technology centers sponsored by Comsoft, and thus is indebted to all the participants in these events. It has benefited from the cooperation, encouragement, and prodding of Marjan Bace and Lee Fitzpatrick at Manning Publications Co., and the production assistance provided by Aaron Lyon. Finally, special thanks go to the families of the authors for encouragement and support in making this book a reality.

TIMOTHY D. KORSON
VIJAY K. VAISHNAVI

chapter 1

The goals, activities, and organization of an object technology center

Introduction

An object technology center (OTC) is a technology transfer center that specializes in the rapid development and deployment of the infrastructure necessary to successfully use object-oriented software development techniques on a corporate scale.

OTCs are a relatively new corporate phenomenon.[1] The first organized meeting for members of OTCs was a workshop at OOPSLA'93. Since then the OTC workshop series has become an annual event at OOPSLA. In addition, a series of conferences[2] dedicated to members of OTCs has been established. Through these meetings we have identified numerous corporations that have an OTC. Four of these corporations (IBM, BNR, The Travelers, and Wiltel) are contributing whole chapters to this book. Seven other OTCs are contributing summary information.

These workshops and conferences serve as a valuable forum for information exchange and collaboration. New attendees often remark that before attending they were not aware of how many other companies had a formal OTC.

Organizationally, OTCs span the spectrum, from grassroots organizations to formal committees to funded entities. Among the funded entities, some get up front funding, while others get paid for services they deliver to specific projects. Their sizes range from a single person to a staff of over thirty. The projects they support range from pilot projects of 2–3 people, to mature 1000-person projects.

The OTCs represented in chapters 2–6 are representative of this diversity. Some of them represent the larger and more mature OTCs. Other chapters describe smaller OTCs.

In the rest of this chapter we will describe, in generic terms, the goals, activities, and organization of an object technology center. The middle chapters are case studies written by the heads of the OTCs represented. Chapter 6 presents summary information from seven other OTCs. The last chapter will synthesize the case studies and relate them back to the generic material presented in this chapter.

The goals of an OTC

The goals of an OTC are derived from its mission as a technology transfer center. Figure 1.1 shows a simple OMT object model of technology transfer. Each association class in the model relates to a major OTC goal:

- drive acceptance of object technology

- ensure success of projects using OT

- transfer expertise to the development staff

- mature the OO process being used by the corporation

- define effective roles for projects using OT

- assist with the selection of pilot OO projects

  Each of these goals is elaborated below.

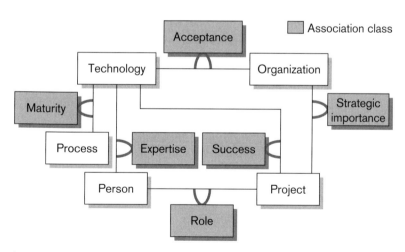

Inspired by the IBM presentation given by Geoff Hambrick at the OOPSLA'94 workshop on OTCs.

Figure 1.1   Object model of technology transfer

Figure 1.2　Technology–organization goals

Drive acceptance of object technology

An OTC must understand the theoretical merits of OT and must be able to present them in a compelling manner to both management and members of the technical staff. To do this well, an OTC must devote resources to the preparation of seminars and presentations on OT (see Figure 1.2). However, an organization will typically not accept object technology on the basis of its theoretical merits alone. The most effective means of driving acceptance of OT is by demonstration. Thus one of the first activities of an OTC is the nurturing of a successful pilot project that can be used to demonstrate the benefits of OT. Case histories and anecdotes of the use of OT in other organizations will never suffice to address the concerns of skeptics within the organization. There is always some level of belief that "our organization" is unique. Thus an initial task of an OTC is to demonstrate in-house both the feasibility and benefits of OT.

Ensure success of projects using OT

As noted above, an OTC usually has a special relationship to a pilot project and a few select initial projects. Beyond these special relationships, which are related to the goals of the previous section, an OTC has a direct goal of ensuring the success of all projects using OT (see Figure 1.3). The OTC does this by housing a staff of experienced mentors that can be loaned to projects without sufficient staff experience in OT. In

Figure 1.3   Technology–project goals

addition the OTC is responsible for creating the infrastructure necessary to support projects using OT. This includes the production of a variety of process handbooks. In fact, most of the activities of an OTC revolve around direct project support.

Transfer expertise to the development staff

In Figure 1.4 the focus is on the transfer of OT expertise to the software development staff. This goal both overlaps and conflicts with the previous goal. It overlaps in that transferring OT skills to project personnel helps ensure the success of the projects to which they are assigned. It conflicts in that the learning curve for OT often requires a longer time frame than what project deadlines can accommodate. Thus OTC mentors are often torn between assuming the technical lead role on a project to help ensure quick project success versus assuming a teaching role that maximizes the learning of project staff. Thankfully these goals are not always at odds. A skillful mentor can often teach OT skills while guiding the development staff towards a quality project design.

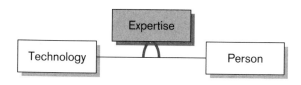

Figure 1.4   Technology–person goals

Managers must not be neglected in this process. Most managers will need an OTC management consultant to assist them with project planning and tracking, and team organization for the first few iterative/incremental OT projects they manage.

Mature the OO process being used by the corporation

The process maturity model defined by the SEI is used by a growing number of organizations to characterize the maturity of their software development processes and to guide them in the progression from one level to the next. When an organization first adopts OT, it is typically for a fairly small project which can be driven from a design and technological point of view. However, as an organization starts to use OT on larger projects, process starts to play an increasingly important role. Since OT represents a fundamental paradigm shift in process, organizations typically find themselves at SEI level 1 for the initial projects. These initial projects usually encounter the typical problems of a project using a level 1 process. These problems lead the organization to undertake an effort to move to higher levels of process maturity for OT. In fact, many OTCs are organized at this point of adopting OT. In this case, the OTC charter includes a clear mandate to formalize and mature the process for OO software development (see Figure 1.5).

Figure 1.5   Technology–process goals

CHAPTER 1:   GOALS, ACTIVITIES, AND ORGANIZATION

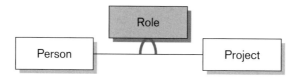

Figure 1.6 Person–project goals

Define effective roles for projects using OT

Organizations moving to OT often do so as a part of a fundamental change in the way they develop software. These changes include:

- a focus on component identification and reuse

- increased use of prototyping for risk reduction

- a life-cycle approach to testing and quality assurance

- an approach to system architecture that relies on pattern identification and composition

- the development of application frameworks and domain-specific pattern languages

These changes are often treated as an integral part of OT, and the OTC is given the responsibility of helping propagate these changes throughout the organization. One way in which an OTC does this is to define effective roles for projects using OT (see Figure 1.6). OTCs typically also help managers create project organizations that effectively use these new roles. These new roles often include:

- system architect

- architectural review board

- reuse coordinator

- component and pattern librarian

- project and team test prime
- prototyper

Assist with the selection of pilot OO projects

Organizations starting out with OT are often far too ambitious. One of the critical goals of an OTC is to ensure that this ambition is tempered with reality. Figure 1.7 depicts the fact that each project has some strategic importance to an organization. This strategic importance is related to a number of factors. The most important factor is typically the business value of the software product under development. This is not, however, the only factor. Many times a project takes on a strategic importance related to the perceived importance of the technologies being used to develop the system. An all-too-common error of an organization is to take a group of software developers skilled in one set of technologies and put them on a strategically important software system using multiple new technologies. As an example consider a team of developers skilled in PL/I and DB2 running on an IBM mainframe. To ask this team of developers to undertake the development of an object-oriented system using client/server techniques on a network of Suns and PCs with a graphical user interface, and then add a tight schedule for a mission critical project, is to ask for failure. On the other hand, if OT is only used for minor projects with little strategic importance, OT will never gain the visibility needed for larger scale support. Thus a specific

Figure 1.7   Organization–project goals

goal of an OTC should be to ensure that the right projects are selected, and that projects doomed to failure are rejected for use as an OO pilot project. An alternative to rejecting doomed projects is to work with management to remove the high risk factors that make the project likely to fail.

OTC interactions

Figure 1.8 describes OTC interactions with other parts of the corporation. The most obvious interaction on the diagram is that an OTC must support projects using OT. The OTC support role for projects is elaborated later and includes providing mentors, supporting reuse, documenting the corporate process, etc. The next most obvious interaction is with upper level management, which must be lobbied for financial and political support for OT. The most often overlooked interaction is with peer organizations within the corporation. Most corporations have a formal process group, a metrics group, a testing group, a general technology transfer group, and other

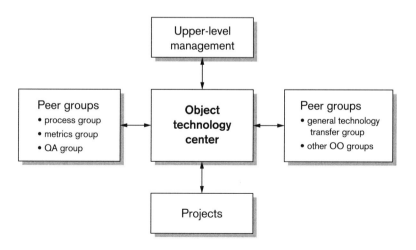

Figure 1.8   Object technology center interactions

OO groups within the corporation. An OTC needs to nurture interaction with each of these groups. The corporate process group needs to understand the impact of incremental/iterative techniques on the process of software development. The metrics group needs to have support in understanding how to measure the complexity of OO designs and the productivity of developers using OO techniques. The testing group needs to know how inheritance and polymorphism affect unit and cluster testing, and how incremental delivery affects black-box acceptance testing. If an OTC fails to elicit the cooperation and support of these other corporate groups, they will often find themselves in political difficulty due to the opposition of the other corporate groups to the policies the OTC is recommending. As a consultant to OTCs, one of the activities we often engage in is to hold meetings with managers of these peer organizations to explain the impact of OT to their area of concern.

One of the key relationships of an OTC is its relationship to other corporate technology transfer groups. Most companies have at least one group that is charged with examining new technologies for potential use within the organization. Often these technology transfer groups are also charged with the infusion of selected new technologies into the corporation. In this situation there is a potential overlap of responsibilities between the general technology transfer group and the OTC. Because of this overlap some corporations have attempted to make the OTC simply a "working group" within the general technology transfer group. This does not work well. Our recommendation is that an OTC should constitute an organizationally separate entity. When an OTC is part of a larger technology transfer unit, OT is too often seen as just another implementation technology, on a par with, and potentially, politically competing with, for example, client-server technology. In such an environment OT can never really be exploited to its full extent. Obviously OT includes an implementation technology, but OT is also widely recognized as a fundamental paradigm shift in the process of software development. As such, OT needs to have its own special support team: the OTC. Because of these reasons, many corporations do, in fact, have both an OTC and a general technology transfer group. In this case care must be taken that each group understands its relationship to the other. This can and should be done formally within the written charter for each group. However, as a practical matter, the heads of the groups need to have a good working relationship together. Generally the division of concerns is related to the time horizon involved. The OTC is concerned with the immediate and near term. The general tech transfer group is concerned with longer term issues and technologies. So, for example, the creation of a handbook of immediately applicable domain-specific design patterns would fall to the OTC. Exploration of a next-decade project, using intelligent agents running on massively parallel processors, would fall to the technology transfer group.

Other OO groups besides the OTC may exist within an organization. This could include groups creating OO CASE tools, OO consulting groups, and even an OO methodology group. This does not often occur in small companies, but we have worked with companies which simultaneously had a group working on a methodology and supporting CASE tool, an internal group selling OO consulting services to external clients, multiple groups developing OO products (e.g., C++ compilers, class libraries, OODBMSs, etc.) for the marketplace, and an internal OTC. Obviously such an organization would need to devote time and energy to maintenance of the complex interactions between these groups. To neglect these interactions is to risk treading on someone's political turf and getting reorganized out of existence.

Setting up an OTC

Setting up an OTC (see Figure 1.9) usually requires the support of several corporate champions of your cause. You will need at least one highly respected member of the technical staff and one high-level manager to support your efforts. The person attempting to establish the OTC can sometimes double as the technical champion, but you will need committed management support. One test of the management support for a corporate OTC is whether the company is willing to join Comsoft,[3] the consortium of OTCs. An organization that is serious about establishing an OTC will want to attend the annual OTC conferences, receive the OTC newsletter and handbooks, and participate in other Comsoft activities. Once there is sufficient support for an OTC, a business strategy and organizational plan needs to be established.

- Find a corporate champion
- Join Comsoft, the consortium of OTCs
- Write up your business justification and funding strategy
- Create and prioritize a set of goals and activities
- Create an organizational structure for the OTC complete with a review board
- Recruit the needed personnel—include someone experienced in tech transfer and object technology
- Have an outside audit every 6 months

Figure 1.9   Setting up an OTC

Funding models

Figure 1.10 depicts three different funding models. Model 1 is the most common model we have seen. The centralized, up-front funding of model 1 is consistent with the infrastructure

	Model 1	Model 2	Recommended
Source:	Centralized	Distributed	Blend
Timing:	Up front	Chargeback	Blend
Scope:	Single family of projects	Many diverse projects	Focus on an area, but larger scope

Figure 1.10   Funding models

mission of an OTC. The danger, however, is that an OTC funded this way can lose touch with the real needs of the projects it is supposed to be supporting. The distributed, chargeback funding of model 2 keeps an OTC focused on the real needs of projects but risks turning the OTC into simply an internal consulting group. The recommended funding model combines centralized, up-front funding with distributed, chargeback money. This blend allows an OTC to pursue infrastructure, technology transfer roles in a planned manner while making sure that the OTC is responsive to the corporate bottom line.

Business justification

Whatever funding model is chosen, costs and benefits need to be quantified and presented as a part of a well-thought-out business case. OTC visionaries are often reluctant to quantify costs and benefits because of the uncertainty involved (see Figure 1.11). Nevertheless, without a clear financial model of why an OTC makes business sense, an OTC is always on shaky ground and dependent on the whim of management for continued funding. Quantification of costs is not difficult. Quantification of benefits is based on savings from reduced duplication of effort, decreased time to market for well-supported projects, and increased quality of products

- Quantify costs and benefits
- Quantification can be in:
  - dollars
  - time to market
  - quality

Figure 1.11 Funding strategies

produced with a more mature process, etc. Dollar amounts can be assigned for each of these areas and input into the OTC financial model. These dollar amounts will be based on a set of "soft" assumptions which should be clearly documented and periodically reviewed for continued validity and accuracy. Because these "soft" assumptions cannot be proved, and may frequently be off by as much as an order of magnitude, many OTC organizers are reluctant to create financial models based on them. It has been our experience that this reluctance does not serve an organization well. Financial models need to be created so that we have something against which to track financial reality. Financial modeling is like project planning. The original estimate may be way off, but the model allows us to track actual progress against projections and thus have a basis for management action.

At one of our consulting sites (see Figure 1.12), each team manager agreed to lend a person to the OTC staff according to a negotiated rotation schedule. This tangible evidence of

- Each team manager agreed to lend a person to the OTC according to a negotiated rotation schedule
- Project leader's buy-in helped convince management to fund the OTC

Figure 1.12 BNR staffing model

CHAPTER 1: GOALS, ACTIVITIES, AND ORGANIZATION

project leader's buy-in helped convince upper management to fund the OTC. In this case, the business justification revolved around the fact that each team's progress was being impeded by a lack of a general infrastructure. Many process issues needed to be resolved for the proper coordination of the multiple teams involved in the project. The team leaders were willing to quantify the worth of the OTC to them by the amount of time they were willing to lend a team member to the OTC.

Organizational structure and staffing

Some of the corporations we work with have a centralized OTC that supports multiple sites, but most of the OTCs we know of are distributed. To be effective we find that an OTC needs a physical presence at locations it wishes to influence. When staffing an OTC, a number of positions need to be considered (see Figure 1.13). Some of these positions are only relevant to a large formal OTC (e.g., the board of directors). A small OTC may have only 1–3 employees, but most of these staff roles still need to be filled, even if one person fills multiple roles. A small OTC may also elect to contract out some of the roles, or to collaborate with other existing departments (e.g., the training department) for the fulfillment of these roles.

- Board of directors
- Director
- Mentors
- Reuse staff
- Process staff
- Quality assurance staff (metrics, testing, OO design)
- Training coordinator (and staff?)
- Coordinator for tool acquisition and vendor relationships

Figure 1.13   Staffing a centralized OTC

Board of directors   The board of directors is needed to keep an OTC on track. As certain goals are achieved, and as the organization gains experience with OT, the prioritization of the goals and activities of an OTC should change. The board of directors should require the OTC director to periodically furnish the board with an updated financial model as well as a set of prioritized goals and objectives. The board should also monitor OTC interactions with the other peer organizations in the corporation. Board members should include:

- a representative of upper management

- the head from at least 1 peer organization (e.g. the quality assurance center) within the corporation

- project managers from several of the key projects being supported by the OTC

- the head of an OTC from another corporation

- the person[*] with the most OO expertise in the corporation

- the director of the OTC

- the best OO consultant you can find

Director   The director of the OTC has the standard responsibilities relative to the board of directors and the overall success of the OTC. The most frequent error we have seen made in the selection of an OTC director is to hire a manager with no OO expertise, or to hire an OO guru with no management experience. The OTC needs a head with both management experience and OO expertise. The problem is that such individuals are currently in short supply in most companies. Because of the direct bottom line contribution and visibility of individual projects, corporations sometimes assign the most experienced OO managers to critical projects, leaving the slot

---

[*] Not employed within the OTC.

of OTC director to be filled by a manager with little or no significant OO experience. We often find this situation but this is backwards. A good project manager with little OO experience can lead a very successful project with the assistance of an OO management consultant from the OTC or from a good outside consulting group. The OTC will not fulfill its potential without a manager with significant OO expertise.

Mentors   Mentors should be good teachers as well as OO experts. A large OTC will maintain an internal staff of mentors. A small OTC will maintain a list of certified OO consultants that projects can contract with for mentoring services. In this case it will be the responsibility of the OTC to coordinate the external vendors so that a consistent philosophy, process, and methodology is conveyed to projects within the company. This philosophy must be consistent with the handbooks being developed by the OTC. Mentoring is one of the four core activities of an OTC and as such is further elaborated later in this chapter.

Reuse staff   Some OTCs have no reuse staff, and others have a number of persons dedicated to reuse. Most of the existing OTCs that have a reuse staff are in a company that also has another separate reuse group. This overlap of responsibility could lead to turf wars, but could equally well lead to collaboration. Generally the OTC reuse staff focuses on OO-specific reuse, such as class library issues, OO frameworks, and OO design pattern reuse. The OTC reuse staff can then collaborate with any existing reuse groups on general reuse issues. A common mistake made in staffing these positions is to get persons with OO experience but no general reuse expertise. As another of the four core activities of an OTC, supporting reuse is further explored later in this chapter.

Process staff   Persons working on the corporate OO process should be realists. We have heard many managers and developers comment: "we are processed out." It is very easy to produce a process handbook that requires projects to maintain mountains of documentation. The process staff should realize that there is not one process that is applicable to every project. This implies that the process staff should be careful to annotate each step/activity/document with the conditions that indicate that a project should include that step/activity/document in the process for that project. It is all too easy for a process person, sitting in an office at corporate headquarters, to make unrealistic demands on a project team. We know of one OTC that created a process that required the creation of a state transition for *every* class in the system. The system under development had many passive classes for which the creation of a state transition diagram was simply busy work, but the project manager was under pressure to follow that OTC process, so the busy work was done. As a result the OTC received a bad name.

Quality assurance staff   The quality assurance staff will be responsible for the creation of a quality assurance plan that includes continuous reviews, audits, and testing. The quality assurance staff may also work with the process staff on ISO certification and implementation.

Training coordinator   A large OTC will typically have a training coordinator. It may also have a training curriculum and staff for training on internal frameworks, processes, etc. The training coordinator should also certify external vendors that wish to supply OO training within the company. A small OTC would typically collaborate with the corporate training center for this function.

Coordinator for tool acquisition and vendor relationships The coordinator for tool acquisition should certify a compatible set of tools that are preferred and supported by the corporation. CASE tool evaluation is a difficult task. Every vendor wants to sell you the "next version" of their product, because the current version doesn't have everything you require. A basic problem is that expectations and pricing for tools far exceed the value of what current tools actually deliver. We know an OTC that, because of this, has spent over a year in tool evaluation and still has not selected a tool. If an organization is committed to waiting for, or building internally, the ideal tool, then the coordinator for tool acquisition should certify some low-cost temporary solution for immediate use. There are some shareware tools available that, coupled with a document processor such as Framemaker, can provide a good temporary solution. In fact, some OTCs recommend these low-cost shareware tools as the preferred CASE solution. We have seen this work quite well when coupled with a comprehensive design prototype.

Goals and objectives

It is important that an OTC define and prioritize a set of goals and objectives. The board of directors, which should include the head of an OTC from another corporation, should periodically review these goals and objectives as a part of the process of managing the OTC.

A problem we frequently identify at a given OTC is that as it begins to engage in more and more good activities (see Table 1.1), the OTC neglects to relate them back to a clear set of prioritized goals and objectives. In this case the OTC may quickly find itself overextended in the wrong direction. To effectively serve an organization, an OTC must be managed. Many existing OTCs have a director to manage the activities of the OTC, but lack a process for managing the OTC itself. In practice we find that not all OTCs should share the same set of goals. As the consortium for OTCs, Comsoft has found that there is a common framework for a well-run OTC, but that specialization is needed.

Table 1.1 OTC activities—survey results from 11 OTCs[a]
• primary activity   + secondary activity

Activity	IBM	BNR	BOE	EDS	JPM	ITT	LOF	UOL	MM	TI	TRV
Education/knowledge broker	•	•	+	•	•	•		•	•	•	+
Build book library	+		+	•	+	+	+	+	+	+	+
Newsletters	+	+	+		+				+		
Seminars	+	+	+	+	+	+		•	+		•
Mentoring	•	+	+	•	•	•		•	•	+	•
Support pilot projects	•	+	+	•	•	•	+	•	+	•	•
Apprenticeships	•			•	+				•		•
Object-oriented hot line	•	+	+	+							
Customizing technology for projects	•		+	•		+		•	•		+
Monitoring project status	+			+	+			•	+	+	+
Drive cross-project information	•	+		+	•	•		+	•	+	•
Infrastructure for cross-project use	+	+			•	•		+		+	+
Change organizational culture	•	+		+	•	+	•	•	+	+	•
Reuse management	+			+	•	•	+	+		•	+
Manage vendor relationships		+	+		•	+	+				+
Tool acquisition and licensing		•	+		+	+	•	+			+
Tool evaluations	+	•	•	+	+		•	•	+	•	+
Ensure unified view from consultants		+	+		+	•	+			+	+
Business strategy synchronization			•	•	+	+	•	+			•
Evaluate class libraries	•		+	+	•	•	•	•			
Justify object technology center	•	+	•		•	•		+		+	
Build common view of architecture			+	+		•	+	•		+	+
Contribute to state-of-the-art	+	+		•		+		•			+
Develop custom methods	•	•		•		+		+			+
Develop reusable frameworks			+	+	•	•					+

CHAPTER 1: GOALS, ACTIVITIES, AND ORGANIZATION

Table 1.1   OTC activities—survey results from 11 OTCs[a] (continued)
• primary activity   + secondary activity

Activity	IBM	BNR	BOE	EDS	JPM	ITT	LOF	UOL	MM	TI	TRV
Develop handbooks	•	•		•	+	+	•	•			+
Coding guidelines	•	+		+	•	+	•	+	+		+
Reuse guidelines	•	•		+	•	•	+	•		•	+
Management presentations	•	+	+	•		•		+		+	
Promote company activities externally	+	+		+	+					+	
Lobby for support of technology	•		•	+	+	+	•	•	+	+	

a. IBM, Bell Northern Research, Boeing, Electronic Data Systems, J.P. Morgan, ITT Hartford Insurance, Libbey-Owens Ford, University of Linz, Martin Marietta, Texas Instruments, The Travelers

Activities

There are many legitimate activities which fall within the scope of an OTC. Table 1.1 summarizes the activities of OTCs as reported at the OTC workshop held at OOPSLA'94. This matrix forms a basis for comparison of activities across OTCs. Each of the OTCs represented in Chapters 2–6 of this book have filled in this matrix. In the last chapter we use this matrix as a basis for comparison and analysis.

We have found that in practices the most important of these activities can be categorized into four core areas (see Figure 1.14).

Making object technology work for your organization— four core activities of an OTC

• shielding projects from corporate politics
• mentoring and apprenticeships
• creating and distributing handbooks
• supporting reuse

Figure 1.14   Core activities

Shielding projects from corporate politics

Each individual project should not have to fight all of the corporate politics it takes to make an OO project successful. The OTC should shield the individual project from these higher level issues. In this protectorate role, an OTC should:

- convince management that OT is viable

- get process waivers

- fight the "iterative process versus waterfall funding" battle

- get metrics waivers so that OO projects are not evaluated on LOC measures

- lobby for support of investment in training, mentoring, tools, etc.

- get tool waivers so that the OO projects do not have to use the corporate-mandated, structured analysis CASE tools

Shielding projects from corporate politics is one of the first tasks of an OTC. Until management is convinced that OT is viable, and the first pilot project is started, the rest of the activities of an OTC are irrelevant. As OT becomes an accepted, better understood, corporate technology, the amount of time an OTC devotes to this role will diminish.

Mentoring and apprenticeships

An OTC must house, or at least collaborate with, the best OT expertise in the corporation, or it will not be respected and correctly utilized. On the other hand, the OTC must be careful not to develop the attitude of an elitist organization. In practice, this is a frequent and serious problem. We have seen numerous times when a project team refused good counsel from an OTC mentor because of the mentor's know-it-all attitude.

Mentoring is such an important task of an OTC that we are surprised at how many OTCs neglect the instruction and nurturing of their mentors. A support program for the OTC mentor should include:

- formal instruction on mentoring techniques

- an apprenticeship program for training future mentors

- ongoing advanced OO training for mentors and funding for attending conferences

- a planned forum for interaction amongst the mentors

- time for formalizing and documenting the techniques and heuristics they use

An OTC must plan on turnover amongst the mentors. If you succeed in developing a good team of mentors, you will make them more valuable than your company will be willing to pay them. Experienced OO consultants are in demand, and you should plan on a percentage of your mentors leaving the company to become independent consultants. In fact, in a paradoxical sort of way, one measure of the success of your mentoring program is how many of them leave your company to become independent consultants.

Besides the apprenticeship program for training future OTC mentors, the OTC should establish an apprenticeship program for project team members who wish to acquire additional OO expertise. The program is a win–win situation. The OTC wins in that it now has additional personnel with which to accomplish its tasks. The projects win in that their team members get concentrated exposure to OT as it is practiced within the corporation. Such apprenticeships should be at least 60 days long.

One of the featured topics at a recent OTC workshop was mentoring. The J.P. Morgan and IBM OTCs gave reports focusing on advice (see Figure 1.15) and things to avoid (see Figure 1.16) based on their experience in this area.

- Get management team involved early
- Make a contract with the project team—different teams have different needs
- Clearly establish mentor roles and responsibilities
- Allow object center personnel to perform multiple functions
- Provide **documented** tools, techniques, and rules of thumb
- Drive mentoring approach from real work products
- Document and evaluate mentoring process
- Keep an ongoing training program for mentors
- Accept apprentice mentors

Based on recommendations from the OOPSLA OTC Workshop '94

Figure 1.15   Mentoring advice

- Subjective arguments between mentors
- Treating all projects the same
- Not adapting to the increasing expertise of a project staff over time
- Mentoring faster than the project team can assimilate the information
- Painting an unrealistic picture of the technology without discussing costs and risks
- Don't confuse a mentor's role with that of an internal contractor
- Don't be seen as an elitist organization

Based on recommendations from the OOPSLA OTC Workshop '94

Figure 1.16   Mentoring things to avoid

Creating and distributing handbooks

OT is commercially viable, but because OT is still an immature technology, OTCs need to contribute to the state of the practice. In addition, an OTC will need to customize and integrate OT into the culture and infrastructure of the organization. The results of these efforts should be codified into handbooks. OTCs typically produce handbooks in a number of areas (see Figure 1.17).

CHAPTER 1:   GOALS, ACTIVITIES, AND ORGANIZATION

Figure 1.17   Creating and distributing handbooks

Process   A corporation typically starts with one of the commercial methodologies such as Rumbaugh, Jacobson, or fusion. Projects typically find out that a blend of the methodologies works best for them. Yet blending methodologies should not be done in an ad hoc manner. The OTC should formalize and document the local blend. This situation is complicated when the implementation environment is not pure OO. Many corporations are using a client-server implementation environment such as Powerbuilder, Forte, or Delphi. In this case the "pure" OO methodologies need to be blended with the client-server methodology of the implementation environment.

Once an OTC has a methodology worked out, it will find that it now must address the larger issue of a comprehensive software development process which includes issues in requirements gathering, deployment, field support, quality assurance, and ISO 9000 certification.

Developing a corporate OO software development process typically consumes a large percentage of OTC time and resources.

Testing   Object-oriented design techniques bring a whole new set of factors to bear on the testing process. For example, consider the impact of inheritance on component testing. The iterative/incremental process affects the interaction between the independent test team and the development team. While it is true that from a black-box system testing perspective, one doesn't care what kind of technology has been used to develop the system, the use of OT does have a substantive impact on the testing process.[4] The OTC will need to elaborate and communicate this process to the development team.

Metrics   Managers use project metrics to plan and track project resource needs. Managers use product metrics to access the quality of software systems. There is a general lack of understanding of both product and process metrics for OO systems. Yet managers have an immediate need to be able to plan, track, and assess the quality of software systems built using OO techniques. An OTC needs to capture and track the best current practice in OO metrics and communicate this to project managers. This is an area in which an OTC will need to work closely with industry research consortia such as Comsoft.

Design guidelines   The mentoring staff of the OTC should document the design guidelines and heuristics they use when mentoring projects. These guidelines should be assembled into a design handbook, categorized, and examined for consistency. By making it a part of the standard design review process, this design guidelines handbook can be used to leverage the mentors' knowledge across the corporation.

The role of Comsoft in developing handbooks   One of the primary activities of Comsoft is the creation of generic handbooks which can quickly be specialized by member OTCs. Comsoft has handbooks in most of the above areas.

> - An OTC should own a library of reusable classes and frameworks (this is an excellent way to provide an apprenticeship program for your organization)
> - Some OTCs create frameworks and components
> - Many OTCs evaluate commercial class libraries and reuse tools
> - An OTC should provide a handbook on reuse

Figure 1.18 Supporting reuse

Supporting reuse

As indicated in Figure 1.18, many OTCs own a library of reusable classes and frameworks. The creation and maintenance of this library can be an excellent way for the OTC to provide apprenticeship opportunities to those in the corporation wishing to gain experience in class design, development, and reuse.

There are two primary ways to achieve effective apprenticeships within an OTC. One is to serve as a direct apprentice to a specific mentor and to assist and observe that mentor. The second is to join the OTC reuse team and, under the direction of a senior designer, assist with the development and evolution of reusable assets.

Some OTCs also create and own domain-specific frameworks. Many OTCs evaluate commercial class libraries and reuse tools. As indicated in the previous section, an OTC should provide a handbook on reuse.

Other supplemental activities

One of the roles of an OTC is to be a center of expertise for object technology. Activities related to this role include:

- maintaining an "OO hot line"

- housing a library of key books, journals, and internal tech reports

An analysis of the OOPSLA OTC Workshop reports reveals the following additional kinds of activities of an OTC:

- center of expertise

- manage tool acquisition and vendor relationships

- promote company activities externally

Figure 1.19 Other activities

- hosting seminars

- publishing an internal newsletter (see Figure 1.19)

Other supplemental activities include managing tool acquisition and vendor relationships as well as promoting company activities externally.

Types of OTCs

An analysis of the many OTCs we have worked with shows that they tend to cluster into two different types of OTCs:

- consulting groups

- infrastructure groups

Obviously there is overlap, but the difference in focus between the two types of OTCs is noticeable in the funding models, organizational structure, staffing levels for different staff categories, and written mission statement.

Corporate consultants

OTCs in this category devote most of their staff positions to mentoring and training. Funding for this type of OTC tends

Figure 1.20   Types of OTCs

to be based on the fact that employee consultants are much cheaper than external consultants.

Corporate infrastructure

OTCs in this category focus on reuse, process, and handbook creation. Many of the staff positions may be devoted to obtaining ISO certification for an OO process. The focus is on producing written material rather than on giving verbal advice on specific problems. Funding is based on reduction of duplicated effort, increase in quality, risk reduction, etc. The problem we encounter with this type of OTC is that it can lose touch with reality.

OTC spectrum

Actually there tends to be a spectrum of OTCs (see Figure 1.20) with corporate consultants marking one end of the spectrum and infrastructure OTCs marking the other end.

Life cycle of an OTC

Over time a healthy OTC will change. We have tried to detect a general pattern in the evolution of an OTC, but there doesn't seem to be a single pattern. Each OTC evolves along a path determined by a complex set of factors unique to the organization that it supports. If, however, we move to a high enough level of abstraction, we can group OTCs into 3 categories. All 3 categories share the tendency to progress from the informal to the formal.

Maturing consulting group   Some OTCs focus on the direct mentoring of projects over the entire life cycle of the OTC. In the start-up phase, the focus is on finding qualified mentors and ensuring the success of individual pilot projects. In this phase each consultant has their own favorite notation, set of heuristics, methodology, etc. Consultants disagree with each other and are thus not interchangeable across projects. Over time these OTCs take on the additional task of formalizing their consulting methodology. The consulting staff arrives at some sort of consensus which is documented and provided to client projects. In the maturity stage these OTCs may become meta-mentors, training apprentice mentors in the art of mentoring.

Maturing infrastructure group   Infrastructure groups focus on producing written handbooks. In the start-up phase most of the written material will be in the form of advice, heuristics, lists of approved tools, vendors, etc. Over time this material is synthesized and customized to the organization that the OTC is supporting. Processes become formalized and more comprehensive. In the maturity stage these OTCs may focus on obtaining ISO certification for an OO process, moving the organization to higher levels of the SEI maturity model, and other formal quality goals.

Consulting → infrastructure group   Many OTCs start off as a corporate consulting group and over time evolve to an infrastructure group. Some believe this to be the natural life-cycle of an OTC. We note that this is perhaps the most common life cycle for an OTC, but we do not see it as the only valid life cycle. In the start-up phase for this scenario the focus is on direct project support through mentoring. Over time this direct support is augmented with written material and a focus on reuse and process. In the maturity stage the focus is on obtaining ISO certification for an OO process, moving the organization to higher levels of the SEI maturity model, and other formal quality goals.

Lessons learned

- strive for a formal repeatable process

- don't wait for a formal process before you let your experts mentor

- aim for a mix of short-term tangible results with longer-term idealistic goals. An organization can't go from level 1 to level 5 in six months.

- avoid methodology wars—learn to think in terms of a meta-process

- mentor in pairs to minimize personality problems and improve continuity

- get the best people

- the best technical gurus may not make the best mentors

- pay continuous close attention to corporate politics or you may wind up reorganized out of existence

- external audits of the OTC will save you a lot of grief

- use your board of directors

Comsoft—the meta-OTC

Comsoft serves as an OTC for OTCs. As such Comsoft:

- maintains an inter-OTC forum for the sharing of experiences

- publishes an OTC newsletter and coordinates OTC conferences and workshops

- monitors and coordinates the international research of interest to OTCs

- sorts through the research results, commercial hype, and products

- conducts the basic research needed to fill the gaps where knowledge is lacking

- synthesizes the "good stuff" into usable handbooks, tools, and recommendations

Comsoft is organized under section 501 c(3) of the IRS code as a non-profit research and education corporation. Comsoft originated as a collaboration with AT&T in 1989[3] and has for the past several years been instrumental in helping establish and sustain a number of OTCs.

Comsoft is a leading center for research in applied object technology. It conducts research in object-oriented software development and project management, and it coordinates and monitors current object-oriented research worldwide. However, Comsoft does not do research for the sake of research. Comsoft conducts applied research targeted to the needs of its sponsors only when there is a need for knowledge and techniques that do not yet exist.

More importantly, Comsoft is also a leader in knowledge engineering for technology transfer. Comsoft integrates research results into handbooks, workshops, and other forms ready for immediate use. Comsoft develops tools that automate the incorporation of their research results into an OTC's development process.

The special areas of focus of Comsoft are dictated by the sponsoring OTCs. The first areas to be addressed were testing and metrics. Current areas also include process, reuse, and design. As an example of the research performed by Comsoft for sponsoring OTCs, consider the area of process metrics. Many companies have an interest in function points as a means of expressing the complexity of a software system. The idea is that the development effort is related to the complexity of the system to be developed. The more complex the system, the more resources required to develop the system. The problem is that in the presence of reuse this hypothesis breaks down. If a corporation has an existing framework and supporting classes, it may be able to develop a system measuring 10,000 function points using fewer resources than needed to develop, from scratch, a system measuring 1,000 function points. What is needed then is research on how to measure the effect of reusable assets and combine that measure with standard function point analysis. This is a current area of Comsoft research and exemplifies the applied type of research done by Comsoft.

Summary

We know of numerous organizations that have tried to establish a formal OTC. Many have succeeded, but many have failed. Focusing on recruiting an excellent technical staff for the OTC is a necessary, but not sufficient, condition for the success of an OTC. An OTC is a business entity. In order to succeed it must have a clear set of business goals and objectives along with a plan for achieving those objectives. An OTC must be carefully managed and should aim for a mix of short-term tangible results with longer-term idealistic goals.

References

1 *OTC: The Comsoft Newsletter,* Comsoft, Spring 1995.

2 *OTC'95 Conference Proceedings,* Comsoft, 1995.

3 Tim Korson and Vijay Vaishnavi, "Managing Emerging Software Technologies: A Technology Transfer Framework," *Communications of the ACM,* Vol. 35, No. 9, September 1992, pp. 101–111.

4 John McGregor and Tim Korson, "Integrating the Testing and Development Process for Object-Oriented Software Development," *Communications of the ACM,* September 1994, pp. 59–77.

chapter 2

IBM's object-oriented technology center

TOM KRISTEK, GEOFF HAMBRICK, AND TOM GUINANE

Background and introduction

The Object-Oriented Technology Center (OOTC) was formed in January 1992, within the International Business Machines (IBM) corporation.

IBM is a multinational company that develops, manufactures, and sells advanced information-processing products, including computers, microelectronic technology, software, networking systems, and information technology-related services. The company was founded in 1911 and today has approximately 200,000 people worldwide. IBM has roughly 20,000 software development professionals in its software development divisions. IBM's 1995 revenue was $71.9 billion.

The formation of the OOTC was driven by an executive group called the Software Development Executive Council, which had created an IBM software development strategy. This strategy's purpose was to recommend the necessary steps IBM's software product development groups should take in order to ensure that IBM could remain competitive in the software industry in the 1990's.

The software development strategy covered a range of topics including processes, tools, human resources, and new technologies. The strategy noted the importance of exploring and exploiting promising software technologies within the IBM software development community. In particular, the effective exploitation of object technology was seen as critical to meeting the competitive challenges of the future.

Why object technology?

The reasons for the importance placed on object technology were the kinds of reasons that are presented continually in the literature on the topic. While there was recognition that the technology was still evolving, and that it is far easier to apply it in the wrong way than the right, the executive council viewed the technology as full of promise. The successful results reported by early practitioners within the company furthered this view, showing the potential for high levels of reuse, increased productivity, higher code quality, and reduced maintenance costs.

It was also clear that within the company various groups had begun to make strong business commitments to object technology, and that the same was true of other companies in the industry. What was equally obvious was that these commitments had two components:

- products were being developed that *enabled* the effective use of object technology by other software developers

- product development groups were *exploiting* object technology to increase their development effectiveness

These factors led to the assessment that the industry was moving forward on object technology, and IBM was positioned to lead in that movement.

The proposed solution

The software development strategy was primarily focused on *exploiting* object technology in order to improve the way that software is developed in IBM. The executive council recognized that the insertion of new technology into the broad range of IBM software development shops would require both a push from the top and a pull from the bottom to be effective.

In the case of object technology, the top-down push could be provided by a core team of experts taking a hands-on approach to proactively educating and training the development community on the benefits of object technology, making strong recommendations about how to deploy it, and then helping to implement the plan by hand-holding projects through their first attempts at using object technology.

The bottom-up pull could be effected through a similar approach aimed at providing education and evidence of the technology's value to the development laboratories' technical and management personnel in the hope that they will then want to exploit the technology, and that they will actively seek expert help in doing it. In fact, the pull effect was already working within IBM as the professional curiosity of the software development community concerning object technology was already very high. Teams were looking for help in how to apply it to their projects.

The concept of a technology center of competence was considered the best approach to providing the desired push-pull effect.

This decision was based, in part, on the knowledge that a similar group, called the Reuse Technology Support Center, had experienced some success in its efforts to increase the interest in and practice of software reuse in the company. Beginning in the late 1980's, the reuse center, in conjunction with the Reuse Technology group in IBM Böblingen Germany, was very active in issues of non-object-oriented reuse. Together the groups had established a series of courses on reuse, a library of reusable parts performing core computer science services, a library system for distribution of reusable parts, and a document library covering various aspects of reuse. They also helped to establish reuse site advocates and reuse programs at many IBM locations throughout the world.

The existence of the reuse center not only helped to sell the concept of an object technology center, it also suggested that the same group that had been managing the reuse center should be responsible for getting an object technology center started. That was an organization called System Software Development Tools in IBM Poughkeepsie. Since the group also managed all cross-divisional funding and development of software tools for several years, it was asked to submit a proposal for an object technology center of competence to the Software Development Executive Council.

The proposal that was eventually accepted was to form the Object-Oriented Technology Center (OOTC).

Getting started

The work to create the OOTC began in earnest in January of 1992 when two staff members were asked to lead the effort. The critical first steps in formulating the OOTC were:

- polling sixty IBMers world-wide to ask them what kind of services a group like the OOTC should provide to be of value to them or other groups starting to exploit object technology. The people polled came from a variety of backgrounds including traditional development groups, object technology practitioners, object technology enabling groups, other corporate technology groups, and educators. Published sources outside of IBM were also reviewed.

- visiting key pockets of object technology usage in IBM to understand what they were doing, and what the OOTC could learn from them. The early sites visited included Rochester, Minnesota; Cary, North Carolina; IBM Education in Thornwood, New York; Toronto, Canada; Hursley, England; Böblingen, Germany; Uithoorn, Netherlands; La Gaude, France; Lidingo, Sweden; and Austin, Texas.

- committing the OOTC to be a technical group that provided practical information and support to prospective object technology practitioners and their management at the bottom-up or project level. Strategies for IBM's development and deployment of object-technology-enabling products were not to be an OOTC function. This decision kept the strategy role with other groups already performing it, and allowed the OOTC to focus on *technology insertion*.

- searching for experienced object technology practitioners to staff the group

- formulating an initial pass at the mission and activities that the OOTC would perform

Start-up pains

Getting the OOTC up and functional was not without its minor pains and frustrations. While in retrospect things probably went remarkably well for an undertaking of this scope, there were three primary organizational challenges:

Funding   The OOTC is funded by contributions made by various divisions plus matching corporate grants that come out of a fund set aside in the corporation for support of technology efforts that have cross-divisional application and interest. In 1992, after being commissioned by the Software Development Executive Council, OOTC plans were presented to various executives in a series of meetings that took place over the first seven months of the year. These meetings were aimed at securing their support for OOTC funding. These executives raised numerous questions ranging from the philosophical (Can a a central group ever really be effective at technology insertion?), to the practical (What specific help can you give *my* group?). These questions had to be successfully answered before the first year's budget was granted to the OOTC. The basic answer to those two example questions was that working directly with projects would help keep the OOTC practical and effective, while helping those funding sites successfully deploy object technology.

Funding remains a yearly challenge. Each year the OOTC must ask various divisions for money from their next year's budgets and must also seek the matching corporate grants. Since the OOTC has several years of positive contributions to point to now, the process is a bit easier than it was at the beginning when there was nothing but plans.

Clarifying the mission   Wrapped up in the initial funding discussions was an issue as to whether the OOTC would be encroaching on the missions of product development groups, or other entities that felt that they had some ownership of object-oriented strategies within the corporation. Through repeated refinements of the presentation material, it was demonstrated that helping developers understand how to exploit the technology is fundamentally different from product missions or strategies, and it was a niche that no-one else was filling.

Staffing   Staffing was, and to some extent remains, the biggest concern for the OOTC. Staffing is *the* critical success factor for this type of organization.

To provide the envisioned services required people who not only had a religious fervor that object technology was critical to the future success of IBM's software business, but also a depth of practical expertise that enabled them to help others understand and utilize the technology. What was also desired was diversity in areas of object expertise (i.e., methodology, process, language, tools, education, and metrics), development platforms knowledge, and application domain expertise.

Object technology experts were not in overabundance inside IBM, but they did exist in small pockets throughout the corporation. Through contacts made in earlier jobs, visits to sites active in using object technology, and scanning online object technology forums for recurring names, we were able to identify and locate some of those experts.

Object technology experts and their managers were approached in order to explain the OOTC and to ascertain interest in joining the effort. Experts were sought regardless of their site, with the intent being to have them remain at their home sites under career management of their current managers, but with funding and direction coming from the OOTC. In addition to cutting costs, keeping people at their home sites also provided continued connection to various site object technology efforts (although certainly adding complexity to the day-to-day managing of the OOTC's efforts).

The response to these recruiting efforts was surprisingly successful. On the expert's part, there was extreme interest in doing the consulting work fundamental to OOTC success. On the management's part, these jobs were seen as good career moves with a chance at gaining more experience with the technology and how to help deploy it. Also, it provided a chance for visibility and a chance to move a critical technology into usage throughout IBM. From the beginning of the year, with two people on board to lead the effort, the staff grew to nine by September 1992, with people at seven locations in the United States, Canada, and Europe.

OOTC mission, role, and current goals

OOTC mission and role

The OOTC mission statement was, at the beginning, and remains today, quite straightforward. It is to *facilitate, encourage, and drive the effective application of object technology across the IBM software development community.*

The role defined for the OOTC was:

- to raise awareness of object technology within IBM

- to serve as a point of contact to the IBM internal community for information on object technology

- to increase the level of object technology expertise within IBM

The OOTC has tried to stay true to that mission and that role throughout the life of the group, adding activities or responsibilities to plans only if they seemed consistent with the mission and role.

OOTC current goals

Specific goals in support of the mission are:

- provide high-quality mentoring support throughout the development process

- expand and improve the OOTC document library to cover important aspects of object technology and the object-oriented development process

- increase penetration of OOTC information and other object technology information within the labs

- help development sites create object-oriented support organizations

- promote increased understanding of IBM's object-oriented products and strategies

Some of these goals will be discussed later in the Activities section. The next section outlines how the OOTC is organized and staffed to meet the objectives of these goals.

Organization and staffing

The decision to make the OOTC a technical support organization operating at a project level forced the staffing of the OOTC to be focused on people who had a combination of successful experiences employing object technology to real projects and very good communications skills. The logistics of managing a worldwide group will be discussed in more detail later in this section, but the effect of being a virtual, rather than physical, center means that the OOTC must be well organized in order to fully utilize the available skills of its members.

Organization

The OOTC has three positions defined, all three of which are responsible to provide hot-line assistance to IBMers as needed, as well as author documents on various aspects of object technology. Duties specific to each role include:

1 *Manager*—setting direction and plans, tracking implementation status, budgets, staffing and personnel management

2 *Strategies interface*—interfacing into IBM products and strategies groups; support managers in day-to-day running of OOTC

3 *Consultant*—provide mentoring to OOTC consulting clients; stay current with changes in the object technology field

Since its inception, the OOTC has had 23 different people in the consulting roles. As of this writing there are 12 active members of the OOTC.

Current consulting staff

The general description of the consultant role does not mean that all consultants have the same job, because each consultant has a different area of background and expertise. Since the intent is to assist a wide variety of projects, consulting and documentation assignments are structured to match skills to the job as much as possible. For example, a project that makes a request late in the development cycle may benefit more from consultants skilled in low-level design and code, rather than those skilled in pure analysis.

A high-level look at the current staff follows:

• twelve members

• located in nine sites in seven countries

- range of object technology experience from three years to seven years (4.5 average)

- areas of expertise include:
  - object-oriented analysis
  - object-oriented design
  - process
  - C++
  - metrics
  - tools and environments
  - reuse and class libraries
  - object-oriented education
  - system object model (SOM)
  - object-oriented testing
  - Smalltalk
  - object databases

Logistics

The OOTC has not been given, or sought, the funding to relocate people to one geographic center. Most people in the OOTC are on loan from their home departments for a period of time. Typically this is at least one year, but in many cases several years. They return to that department at the end of the OOTC assignment. During the assignment, consultants are usually with the OOTC full time, but remain available to their departments for high-level technical guidance.

This approach has several advantages:

- not moving people saves time and money

- it is much easier to find willing people when they are not being asked to physically relocate

- most importantly, the majority of consultants come from groups that are very active in some aspect of object technology. Keeping them located with these groups allows them to stay connected to state-of-the art object technology work and also gives access to additional expertise to use within the OOTC.

The biggest drawback to this approach is maintaining healthy, active communications between the far-flung group members. Several means to address this problem have been employed, including:

- an on-line conference disk that serves as the primary vehicle for day-to-day conversations and discussions of work items. For example, all OOTC documents are reviewed on-line by all OOTC members prior to being made available to customers. All comments are seen by all OOTC members, thus ensuring that a document truly becomes an OOTC team effort rather than just the work of one or two people.

- all consulting engagements are also documented in an on-line forum so that consultants not involved in a particular effort can see what others are doing and perhaps offer suggestions or glean knowledge that can be of use to them in their work. This exchange is crucial to the evolution of the mentoring approach.

- monthly conference calls between all team members to quickly touch on status and topics of keen interest

- quarterly full-team meetings that typically last three or four days

- trying to pair every consultant up with every other consultant so that everyone can benefit from the best practices of each other

- occasional technical sub-team meetings where particular people will meet to discuss topics or work items of critical interest

- frequent contact between the team lead and the consultants via phone, notes, or visits

Operating principles

Along with deciding the mission, goals, and organization of the OOTC, an early determination was that all OOTC activities should be based on three basic principles:

- *The OOTC is a bottom-up organization*   This is the key principle. It implies that the OOTC should be staffed by technical personnel, that offerings should be geared to helping individuals and projects, and that the OOTC must be available to offer constructive help and direction in person.

- *OOTC staff, skills, and offerings must evolve as the technology evolves*   Object technology is a broad and evolving topic. This forces a group like ours to continually look for staffing which fills major knowledge gaps, provide the staff the opportunities to stay current, and adjust offerings as changes in the technology warrant.

- *The OOTC must actively solicit and react to user feedback on all of its offerings*   This forces the OOTC to provide feedback mechanisms for all services, aggressively pursue getting that feedback, and alter offerings or approaches as the feedback warrants.

Activities

Categories of requirements

Having gathered requirements from the potential user community, and having built a team to address those requirements, it was realized that to be successful the OOTC needed to offer several types of services across several different groupings of requirements. The requirements that were obtained in the beginning (and those that have evolved since) seemed to fit into three categories:

- *Culture and literacy*—focusing on increasing the awareness of object technology and helping people to understand that education and mentoring need to be carefully positioned in order to successfully use the technology

- *Development process*—addressing the differences in processes that best support object-oriented development and the ones currently being used within IBM

- *Methodology and tools*—concerned with how advances in object technology cause new methods and tools for analysis, design, and programming to emerge

Types of offerings

It was evident early on that the pull effect, discussed in the first section, was in operation because of immediate demands for us to provide not just information on the topics described above, but also assistance in putting the technology into practice. The demand for assistance (both short term and long term) led to the realization that in order to reach more projects, documents would be required to summarize the key concepts as well as offer tips and pointers on various aspects of object technology.

To sustain the pull effect, it was decided that sponsorship of events spotlighting object technology was an effective way of raising awareness in areas that had not yet gotten the message that there might be a better approach to software development than business-as-usual.

This need to satisfy existing requests and keep the cycle going led the group to offer four major services:

1 *Project mentoring* is the most important offering. It requires dedicated time helping designers and developers to learn how to apply object technology and the

related process to a real project. Spending this dedicated time has allowed the OOTC to seed some amount of expertise and experience into the project team through various means:

- recommending educational offerings that development teams should pursue prior to the beginning of the project

- teaching the steps and process for identifying object models at the same time that a good first draft model is developed

- helping to plan project based iteration and prototyping activities in the context of an object-oriented development life cycle

- stepping through the initial designs and prototypes to leave the team with a sense of accomplishment and direction

- staying in touch via phone consultations and follow-up meetings for review of status and technical deliverables

2 *Documents* are written offerings that address various aspects of object technology. The intent is to provide a stand-alone set of information that can be useful to many projects and programmers, since OOTC staffing will never be sufficient to bring this information directly to all people who could possibly benefit from it. Also, it was recognized that producing a set of quality documents would provide a base of OOTC knowledge to use while consulting with projects. This would ensure some commonality in the approach and knowledge that various OOTC consulting teams would take to a site. The following are the guiding principles for OOTC documents:

- they are intended to cover those aspects of the technology and its utilization that are most important to OOTC clients, including such topics as object-oriented maturity; an approach to object-oriented software development;

methodology evaluations; tool and compiler evaluations; metrics recommendations; and education tips and road maps

- the OOTC continually assesses what topics are of prime interest to its customers and tries to react to those interests with useful documents

3   *Assist* is a word used to cover work items that are not as time consuming as consulting engagements, documents, or special events. Assists are recorded in order to provide an idea of how many people are helped in this way. This is reported to OOTC funders, and goals are set each year for the amount of assist support that the team expects to provide. An assist can be many things, including:

- phone calls to handle questions on some aspect of object technology or requests for pointers to information

- visits to a site to present on some aspect of object technology

- requests to remotely review object models, designs, or codes that groups have developed

4   *Events* include OOTC-sponsored object technology conferences, some educational offerings, and presentations on IBM Television

The above are, basically, vehicles for delivering services. Some specific services the OOTC has delivered along with their impact in the customer community are presented next.

Technology transfer through mentoring

Project mentoring is the OOTC's most important and time-consuming offering. This section explores this offering in detail.

Why do mentoring? Almost everyone would accept that the best way to learn something new is by doing it. However, getting started can be difficult because inexperienced teams usually lack both the knowledge and the confidence it takes to do the job. There are three approaches to technology insertion geared towards providing knowledge, or confidence, or both:

- using education to get the knowledge

- using consulting to get the confidence

- using mentoring to get both and more

The role of education in technology insertion Education provides a person or a team an overview-level introduction to the knowledge that it will need to successfully develop a project. Education provides a model of the steps that will be taken during a project. However, education is not a substitute for real experience in avoiding trouble since it cannot warn, or even predict, all of the possible pitfalls and problems that could befall a team as they actually begin to follow that model of steps. Further, the OOTC does not fill an educator's role in the sense that the group does not provide formal classroom training on object technology. Other groups inside IBM have that responsibility. A possible solution to this is to go the next step beyond education to consulting, or to do as the OOTC does and educate informally in the context of mentoring.

The role of consulting in technology insertion In OOTC terminology, a consultant is someone who gets called in to help a project work through particular problem areas in its use of object technology for a short period of time. The consultant is someone who can get the project started on track (or get it back on track), but then moves on. Here a consultant is differentiated from a contractor who would be someone who actually does the project or at least plays a major role in doing the project.

The ability to call a consultant can give a team confidence to strike out on its own, and this makes consulting a valuable service.

A problem with using consultants for technology insertion is that it is not always in the best interest of the consultant to tell the project their secrets of getting out of trouble or staying out of trouble in the first place.

The role of mentoring in technology insertion   The OOTC thinks of its technical staff as mentors. A mentor is part educator, part consultant, and part project advisor.

A mentor may spend some time reviewing or revisiting ideas learned in the classroom, such as analysis and design concepts, but it would be done in the context of the actual project, and the actual approach that the mentor will be showing the project team. This type of education is timely and to the point. It can build from the formal education, but it is being delivered exactly when the project team needs it. It can also avoid causing information overload by teaching the process one step at a time as it becomes needed.

Like a consultant, a mentor is there to help a team through trouble spots, but, a mentor can also recognize danger signs, and warn a team as such signals arise. This helps the team not only to recognize the signals themselves in a real situation, but also helps them avoid the problems in the first place. This is important in leaving the team members with the confidence necessary to take steps on their own. But a mentor should also leave the team members with the feeling that they have a dual safety net; i.e., they should know that the mentor will be back frequently, and they should know that they will have frequent between-visit opportunities to discuss problems with the mentor.

Finally the mentors have a vested interest in providing insights and tips on tricks-of-the-trade so that the team is equipped to do the work. That, after all, is the OOTC mission and is what it is measured on.

Evolution through actual experience   Mentoring goes beyond providing timely education and consulting to the project team because a mentor is truly accountable for the advice and guidance they provide. The fact that the OOTC mentors are evaluated on whether they have helped the team succeed helps to position them as part of the team, thus making their recommendations more credible so that the team is more apt to listen, understand, and act on them in a confident manner.

There is one other reason why the OOTC has focused so much on mentoring as an activity that goes beyond the direct benefits to a project: mentoring provides valuable experience to the mentors. The experience results in two categories of lessons learned:

- those that result in evolving the technology

- those that change the approach to technology insertion

We will leave the subject of technology evolution until later in Lessons Learned, except to say that the experiences that OOTC members gain through mentoring directly affects the quality of all other offerings, especially document offerings, which are updated frequently to reflect the essence of the mentoring practice.

The approach to technology insertion is described in detail in the following subsections.

Summary of OOTC mentoring activity   The OOTC approach to mentoring did not spring forth fully formed upon the creation of the OOTC. In fact, there was not a clear vision as to what exactly the approach would be. But, being that the team was confident that it had more experience and skills with object technology than its prospective clients, it was felt that it was best to start mentoring and let the process evolve as dictated by what the customers said they needed. That process has evolved over time to take advantage of the best techniques used by twenty-three different consultants on actual object-oriented projects over the last three years.

The more than sixty projects mentored by OOTC consultants have covered many different domains, and have tested the ability to widely apply the technology. A few notable examples include systems for:

- accounting and inventory control
- code integration and building systems
- database management
- diagnostics
- system configuration
- real-time phone switching
- network/distribution management
- library control
- information modeling
- plant operations

These projects have presented a broad spectrum of factors that have contributed to the need for different management styles and/or development processes:

- short vs. long schedule
- low vs. high technology risk
- small vs. large project team
- weak vs. firm requirements
- none vs. some experience
- all object-oriented vs. some non-object-oriented code
- all new vs. some legacy code
- iterative vs. waterfall process

Finally, these projects have spanned the globe. A short summary list of IBM sites at which the OOTC has mentored projects is shown below:

- Austin, Texas

- Bethesda, Maryland

- Boca Raton, Florida

- Böblingen, Germany

- Cary, North Carolina

- Dallas, Texas

- Endicott, New York

- La Gaude, France

- Lidingo, Sweden

- Poughkeepsie, New York

- Montpellier, France

- Raleigh, North Carolina

- Rome, Italy

- San Jose, California

- Stockholm, Sweden

- Sydney, Australia

- Toronto, Canada

- Zürich, Switzerland

IBM OOTC approach to mentoring   Working with various kinds of projects under various constraints in locations north-to-south, east-to-west, and A-to-Z, has forced the OOTC to develop an approach that facilitates remote mentoring. The OOTC is committed to getting detailed customer feedback about techniques that worked well during the project, techniques which had no discernible effect, and techniques to avoid in the future. This feedback is crucial to evolving a common and effective OOTC approach. See Figure 2.1 for a high-level diagram of the process.

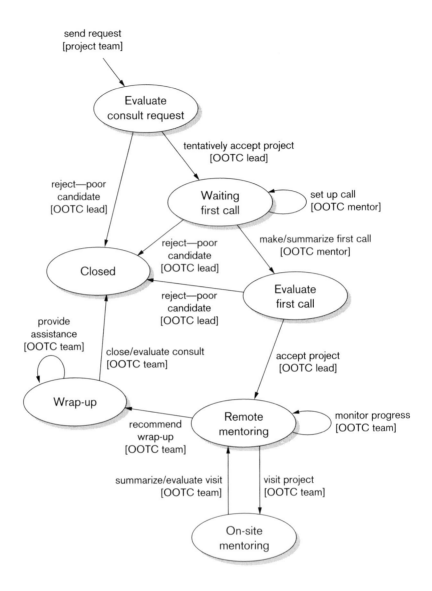

send request
[project team]

Evaluate
consult request

tentatively accept project
[OOTC lead]

reject—poor
candidate
[OOTC lead]

Waiting
first call

set up call
[OOTC mentor]

make/summarize first call
[OOTC mentor]

Closed

reject—poor
candidate
[OOTC lead]

reject—poor
candidate
[OOTC lead]

Evaluate
first call

provide
assistance
[OOTC team]

close/evaluate consult
[OOTC team]

accept project
[OOTC lead]

Wrap-up

recommend
wrap-up
[OOTC team]

Remote
mentoring

monitor progress
[OOTC team]

summarize/evaluate visit
[OOTC team]

visit project
[OOTC team]

On-site
mentoring

Figure 2.1   OOTC mentoring process

Consult request   A typical remote mentoring engagement starts with a detailed consult request from a member of
a development project. The details include domain of the
project, reasons for choosing to use object technology, development and target platforms, language choice, tool choice,

team size, team experience in the domain, team experience with object technology, and project schedules. The first decision point for the OOTC is whether or not the request comes from a product development project in one of the divisions that funds the OOTC. Second, it is considered whether the services requested are services that the OOTC typically provides. Beyond that, the project survey responses are examined to see if there are obvious warning signs that indicate the project is doomed from the start, or that it is not yet ready for a mentor. For example, one request received indicated an impossibly short schedule, and it was rejected as a poor candidate for a transition to object technology. This level of screening can help to avoid object technology being applied in cases where there is no chance for success, thus ensuring that technology is not erroneously blamed for the failure. Unfortunately, once any technology is linked to failure, it is unlikely to be used by that group again.

Another request showed that the project team had no object-oriented training at all and would benefit from a period of formal education before attempting to pilot a project with an OOTC mentor.

First call   When a decision to proceed is made, a first call is placed to the development team to start establishing a mentor relationship. Generally, this is a conference call with one or two OOTC members, the requestor, the team's management, the team leaders, and any other appropriate team members. By having this group of attendees and by assessing how they describe their answers to the survey questions verbally as a team, the OOTC gains a sense of the team's commitment to move to object technology and their willingness to follow OOTC recommendations on things like process. Sometimes OOTC members will ask questions like: "What is your worst fear about moving to object technology?" The answers can be very telling and can help to fine-tune the kinds of services that should be provided to this project, and the approaches that might work best.

After the first call, the OOTC members involved summarize the call and make a recommendation to accept or reject the engagement. Even when a project is rejected as a candidate, the mentoring relationship has begun because in that case some recommendations of a track to follow before making the next request are usually provided to the project team.

First visit   The consultant who initiated the first call is most often the one chosen to lead the engagement, and usually another OOTC member is assigned to the project as well. The consultants are chosen to provide the best possible matches of consultant skills and interest with the project's needs. Having two consultants work with each project is the optimum approach, since:

- it allows a broader spectrum of knowledge and approaches (e.g., perhaps teaming an analysis expert with a person adept in design and implementation)

- mentoring can be draining, and the leadership of the sessions can be shared

- ideas can be bounced between mentors on the fly in order to customize the best approaches and solutions for the particular project

- the person not leading a particular session can be serving as a scribe and also be observing the project team to ensure that individuals are not being left behind by the discussions

The first job of the mentoring team is to plot a course of action that will lead to the FIRST VISIT. The agenda for a typical three-to-four day first visit consists of:

1   an overview of the OOTC services and approach (about an hour)

2   an overview of the project plans and status (about one-half day)

3 a working session depending on the phase, usually consisting of some form of modeling (two or three days)

4 OOTC summary and recommendations to the project team (about two hours)

5 OOTC evaluation to the management team (about an hour)

This is only a guideline. Sometimes a lengthy project overview is dispensed with by reviewing copies of the project documentation (especially requirements and plans) ahead of time.

The goal of the working session is to get the team doing the work as quickly as possible. The OOTC has come a long way since its initial consulting efforts, when it was usually the last day before project team members were able to drive the modeling session. Today, techniques are in use where the project team members are leading the sessions within hours.

For example, during the first visit with a project we'll call the Alpha Project, a technique called *transcribe and converge* was used. The technique is designed so that each team member can quickly get a rough draft analysis model down on paper (transcribe), so that the team can objectively review the models in order to form a consensus (converge). The resulting models were actually quite good, and in this case the team had a good first-draft object model by the end of the second day. The same technique was used to develop dynamic object-interaction models from use cases and scenarios with that initial object model serving as a base. This took one day, and the effort was run almost exclusively by the team members.

The proof of the technology insertion that took place was provided on the last day when the team had a formal in-depth review with an external architecture group. Every member of the team, even the most junior with very little initial domain knowledge, was able to defend the components of the models and walk through the scenarios to resolve issues raised by the architects.

A summary session was then held during which the OOTC recommended that the team continue developing the scenarios to drive out the model, and that another mentoring session be held after it completed the analysis of its top requirements.

In this particular case, the manager attended many of the sessions and actually was a productive participant in the modeling. So the management review was directed more towards the upper management who attended. The activities of the week, what had been developed, how they could be measured and tracked, and what kind of support the team needed from the managers in order to be successful, were discussed.

Although the mentoring visit agendas are usually rather full, an approach that relies on team homework has evolved. This requires both individual and group modeling without OOTC members actually present (although they remain available for questions). This affords ample opportunity for OOTC consultants to huddle, customize the next steps, and summarize the recommendations.

For example, the Alpha Project architecture review practically ran itself, so the OOTC members had plenty of time to develop the summary presentation.

Between visits Project Alpha was an interesting project for many reasons, one of which was that the OOTC used it to pilot a more formal between-visit process than had been used in the past. Before Project Alpha, there was often a laissez faire approach with the mentors waiting for the team members to call with questions and issues. The decision was made to be more proactive between visits. So, the homework concept was expanded, and the team was assigned specific tasks to complete. These assignments were then discussed at weekly conference calls. The idea was to have the team fax the OOTC mentors a copy of the work products (analysis models and scenarios, initially) and have a list of issues and questions ready.

This had a major positive impact in driving the team quickly through the analysis phase. Within 6 weeks the team was ready for design, and a second visit was scheduled.

After each site visit the client is asked to fill out a brief survey on the effectiveness of the visit. Recently, the World Wide Web has been used to post project progress and deliverables for review and discussion.

Second visit   The second visit is patterned after the first, except that the introductory day is not needed. Usually less than an hour is needed to do a status review and to firm the agenda. Most of the time is spent in the working sessions, the content of which depends on the approach used by the consultant.

There are two major approaches that are currently being advocated and followed by OOTC consultants. One is a phased approach where the visits correspond to analysis and design, respectively. The other is a depth-first approach designed to take a narrower slice as deeply into the process as possible, including coding and testing.

There are advantages and disadvantages of both. The phased approach allows for time to build a relatively detailed model during the visit, reduces the chance of information overload, and requires less preparation beforehand. However, it has some down sides as well. It forces a relatively long iteration cycle (18–24 weeks), and teams sometimes have difficulty understanding the analysis work products in the context of the end-to-end process, since they haven't really seen the whole process.

The depth-first approach provides an end-to-end view, giving the team a taste of every activity from analysis through implementation very early in the project development cycle. Site visits using the depth-first approach follow the exact same outline as the phased approach, but consultants using this approach have to work hard ahead of time to make sure that they understand the compliers and other tools used in the development environment in order to insure that a full cycle can be completed in the allotted time. Also, the team members can suffer from information overload if the consultants are not careful to limit the education aspect of the mentoring to just what is needed for the moment.

The Project Alpha engagement followed the phased approach in that the second visit concentrated on a systematic mapping of the analysis model components into a design and an implementation using IBM's VisualAge environment. The OOTC recommendation during the summary was to apply the same rules to the remainder of the model in a systematic fashion and to begin coding from these specifications.

Wrap-up   The typical engagement repeats the between-visit, second-visit pattern until the project is at the end of the design phase. The last visit will usually involve a design review with some basic coding guidelines also being presented. During implementation, the OOTC is available for technical assistance and code reviews. Typically the total number of visits to a team will be five or less.

At this point a final check is done with the project team to see if the request can be closed. If so, they are asked to fill out a detailed evaluation of OOTC services that provides the OOTC with important information on the effectiveness of the entire engagement.

There is also some provision made for staying in contact with the team. For example, after the second visit to Project Alpha, the team created a project forum for issues and questions to which OOTC consultants were subscribed. This facilitated the ability to quickly communicate and reduced the need for the mentors to return to the site.

Preliminary feedback on this project was typical. Teams are generally quite impressed with the mentoring, but they do tend to have some good constructive criticisms. In this case, they would have preferred more coordination between the mentors before the first visit (when sometimes conflicting messages were given); the team also wanted more documentation on techniques used by the OOTC that they could use between visits.

We are using this feedback, and other similar comments, to continue to evolve the mentoring service.

Documents

Documents are one of the primary offerings of the OOTC. Overall, one third of the OOTC's time is spent on efforts related to the development, review, release, and support of documents. The goal is to provide a library of readily available, easy-to use information on a wide range of object technology topics. The documents are based on the experiences of the OOTC, as well as those of other IBM and non-IBM groups. The documents must either provide information that is unavailable elsewhere or must net out information that would require enormous effort for users to sort out individually.

Before being made generally available, each document goes through a rigorous review process inside the OOTC and then is reviewed for usefulness and technical content by at least three non-OOTC members.

All OOTC documents are accessible to any IBMer who has a userid and access to the IBM VNET using a simple REQUEST command. Document availability is publicized in various on-line forums, in presentations by OOTC members, by object technology advocates at various sites, and by IBM education in many of their courses. The documents are now also available on the OOTC home page on the IBM internal World Wide Web site.

The types of documents published by the OOTC have been determined by requirements from its user base. The first set of documents covers fairly basic topics, but later documents have evolved to cover more in-depth topics. The documents themselves are enhanced regularly as the evolution of the technology, or the experience of the OOTC, or its IBM peers dictates.

Earlier, the grouping of requirements into three categories was discussed (Culture and Literacy, Development Process, and Methodology and Tools). The OOTC tries to ensure that these categories are covered by having documents that address different aspects of each category. In each document description that follows the category the document is meant to address is indicated.

The documents available internally include:

- *The OOTC Workbook-Driven Approach to OO Software Development: A Reference Guide*
  - this is the most recent (first released in May, 1994) and most important OOTC document
  - it presents a detailed approach to OO development across the entire life cycle. It is based on (and is a basis for) the OOTC's mentoring offering. It has been updated twice since its initial release and continues to evolve as the OOTC's understanding of OO development matures.
  - in a short time, this document has become the OOTC's second most requested document. This document fits into the Development Processes category.

- *Object-Oriented Analysis and Design Methods: Evaluations and Recommendations*
  - this document presents summaries, evaluations, and recommendations on the major object-oriented analysis and design methods available today. It also provides selection criteria that a team can use in determining which method may be best suited for its project.
  - with over 2,500 unique copies having been requested, this is the most widely distributed document. This points out that within the IBM community there has been a tremendous interest in methods, particularly amongst people looking for assistance in finding the right one.
  - this document is being updated regularly as OOTC experience with various methods grows, and it is moving toward making stronger recommendations on the strengths and weaknesses of the methods

- this document fits into the Methodology and Tools category

- *Object-Oriented Education Road Map*
  - this document consists of a description of various sources of educational information such as courses, video tapes, and conferences. It also presents suggested road maps through the educational offerings depending on skill level and job type.
  - this was one of the first OOTC documents published and remains a widely ordered document since there are still many professionals who are just making the move to object technology today and many others who are looking for very specific courses in detailed technical topics
  - this document fits into the Culture and Literacy category

- *IBM Object-Oriented Maturity Matrix*
  - this is a matrix that development projects can use to help measure their maturity with object technology. It includes steps that can be taken to improve from one maturity level to another.
  - like the education road map, this document has been popular among people just beginning with the technology as it lays out steps that can be taken to move toward proficiency with the technology. It is of particular interest to managers and team leaders as it takes a *project view* of maturity, and discusses how an organization can improve its proficiency in using object technology in its development projects.
  - this document fits into the Culture and Literacy category

- *Object-Oriented Metrics document*
  - this presents a discussion of metrics, and how object technology metrics differ from the ones previously used in IBM. This also lists numerous metrics and describes their potential value with rules of thumb for interpreting them.

○ this has been a difficult topic in that project metrics have been difficult to obtain, thereby making it difficult to arrive at very concrete recommendations for which metrics work and which ones don't. But, efforts in this area continue to be made and the OOTC is now circulating and maintaining tools for the counting of metrics related to C++ and Smalltalk code.

○ this document fits into the Development Process category

- *Reports on C++ compilers, C++ class libraries, and object-oriented tools*
  ○ this contains summaries, evaluations, and recommendations on various C++ compilers, C++ class libraries, and object-oriented tool offerings available
  ○ these documents have proven to be very useful as they provide, in one place, information on the function, portability, cost, support, and internal IBM users of various compilers, class libraries, and tools. Having this level of information accessible to users saves them an enormous amount of research, and allows them to focus on deciding which offering is best for them based on the information provided.
  ○ a downside of producing documents such as these is that they become dated very quickly and therefore need frequent revision
  ○ these documents fit into the Methodology and Tools category

- *Bibliography for Object-Oriented Technology*
  ○ this lists books and papers that OOTC members have found valuable on various object technology topics. The document is structured by topic. For example, all references dealing with methods for object-oriented analysis and design are listed together.
  ○ because of reader feedback, this has evolved toward being an annotated bibliography. The OOTC now makes

strong statements on the usefulness of the material listed in the document.

  ◦ this document fits into the Culture and Literacy category

- *Guidelines for C++ Coding and for Class Library Development*
  ◦ this was the first guidelines document focused on rules of thumb for efficient and effective use of C++ for writing object-oriented applications. A recent guidelines document focuses on rules of thumb for the development of class libraries, and guidelines for ensuring that existing and future class libraries inter-operate well with each other.
  ◦ there is tremendous interest in C++ inside IBM, and the C++ guidelines document is the third most popular OOTC document. Many departments or projects are taking the source for the document and enhancing it with site or project-specific guidelines.
  ◦ these documents could be considered fitting into both the Development Process and the Culture and Literacy categories

- *Usage Guide for IBM's System Object Model (SOM)*
  ◦ this presents an assessment of how best to use SOM, offering examples and rules of thumb
  ◦ this is an example of the documents beginning to advance with the technology, and with the user's interests, into more specific technical topics
  ◦ this documents fits into the Methodology and Tools category

- *OO Testing Handbook*
  ◦ this presents discussion on the best approaches for testing object-oriented software
  ◦ this document fits into the Development Processes category

Twenty thousand copies of the documents have been requested from eight thousand unique userids located at 120 locations worldwide. This represents an undercount, as many people distribute the documents themselves after obtaining them from the OOTC. Additionally, the documents have been viewed over four thousand times in a six month period from the OOTC home page.

As is done with all OOTC offerings, an attempt was made to gauge the impact and acceptance of OOTC documents by surveying all requesters and asking them the simple question: Was the document useful? Additional feedback was encouraged, but the survey needed to be as painless as possible in order to ensure some feedback. The feedback was valuable in ensuring that the documents were useful in general and worth the time that was spent on them. It also provided input that helped redirect future releases of some of the documents. Examples of this include adding strong recommendations to the methods evaluation document and annotating the bibliography.

The survey revealed that 85% of the respondents found the documents useful, 7% did not, and 8% were unsure. Of the people saying that the documents were not useful, many of them cited reasons such as the fact that they were not ready to use a particular document. Very few comments indicated directly that the documents were of poor quality.

The survey led the OOTC to view documents as a beneficial use of time and to institute plans to enhance several of the existing documents.

Documents continue to be treated as a key aspect of what the OOTC does because they not only are useful stand-alone references, but also serve as a common base of knowledge for OOTC consulting activities. These include both the long-term mentoring discussed earlier, as well as the short-term assistance that is discussed next.

Assistance

In some senses the assist support provided by the OOTC is an object-oriented hot line. However, rather than one phone number, there are as many phone numbers for people to call as there are OOTC members. Additionally, an OOTC userid, that is widely known as a contact point into the OOTC, exists for on-line questions.

Since late 1992, the OOTC has tracked the short-term help it provides in a standard format on its conference disk. This was done because members were spending a lot of time providing this type of help, and tracking and reporting it as a legitimate service would allow a full picture of OOTC impact on the user community to be presented to OOTC funders.

Since November of 1992, over 1,000 instances of assistance have been recorded. These have reached 2,100 people inside IBM in a wide range of jobs including designers, developers, managers, planners, and marketing representatives. An optimistic estimate would say that this reflects at most 75% of the actual assistance rendered, as the recording of these sometimes falls through the cracks.

In addition to the normal answering of questions and pointing to sources of information, some of the more beneficial assists have been:

- presenting to many management teams an introduction to object technology that covers terminology, concepts, benefits, risks, how to get started on a first project and what to expect, what to expect on subsequent projects, and usage of the technology inside and outside of IBM

- remote reviews of object models and C++ code

- reviews of plans to start object-technology support organizations at a site

- informal education on analysis, design, and C++ amongst other topics

- supporting site information days on object technology, and presenting various technical topics

The assist offering has been valuable, not only to the people receiving the assistance, but also as a low overhead way for the OOTC to increase its impact and enhance its reputation, thus increasing interest in other, higher-impact offerings such as documents and consulting.

Of course, people who need assistance need to know that the OOTC is an available resource, which is one reason that the group sponsors object-oriented related events. The next subsection discusses OOTC events in more detail.

Events

The primary event offering of the OOTC has been an internal conference on Object-Oriented Software Development. Conferences are very time consuming, so only one was done per year. It is worth noting however that many other events, from educational offerings to site information days, are provided by other organizations in IBM. The positive side of conferences is that they reach many people at once, and they promote an enormous exchange of information between a large cross-section of IBMers with an interest in object technology.

The total number of internal object-oriented conferences held in IBM is now eight, of which three have been sponsored by the OOTC. The OOTC sponsored conferences have chosen locations that have a large number of IBM software professionals in order to ensure a substantial local draw. The eighth conference was actually run by IBM Education and Training, and targeted IBM customers in addition to IBM employees.

The initial conference that the OOTC sponsored was in October of 1992 in Böblingen, Germany. It was co-sponsored with the Advanced Software Technology Group from that site. The conference was fully subscribed with 155 people from 15 countries. There was a wide range of tutorials, technical papers, experience reports, and birds-of-a-feather sessions, as well as external speakers.

The second conference was held in July, 1993 in Toronto, Canada. It attracted 420 registrants from around the world. This number included about 20 IBM customers and business partners on special invitation. The conference was broader in scope than the first one and included two full days of tutorials, a full day of invited speakers from IBM and the industry, and spanned four and one half days in total. The feedback on the conference was very favorable, with 92% of the respondents finding very high value in the offering. 97% of the respondents felt that these types of conferences should continue to be run.

After this second conference, the conference committee conducted a very thorough postmortem which led to many recommendations for improving the conference. These were adopted in the third conference.

The third OOTC conference was held in Santa Clara, California in July, 1994. This third conference lasted five full days and attracted 577 enrollees. That number of attendees exceeded planned capacity, and many potential attendees had to be turned away. This conference included twenty-seven tutorials, two workshops, seven invited speakers, and thirty-five participants in the tools exposition, in addition to the technical papers and panels. There was an increased focus on IBM strategies and object-oriented products, as well as on advanced applications of the technology. This conference drew a 94% favorable evaluation with 99.5% of the attendees saying this offering should continue.

The growth in attendance at the conference, during a time when the overall IBM population has decreased, was a positive message that not only was the offering useful, but also that the interest in object technology from all corners of IBM continued to explode.

The next several subsections will briefly discuss other OOTC activities that don't neatly fall into the four main categories of offerings.

OOTC apprentice program

The basic idea behind all of the OOTC offerings is that there is a logical progression of object technology insertion. This progression takes a group from a relatively immature state which requires a lot of assistance to a state that requires very little assistance and perhaps creates people skilled enough to serve as mentoring resources at their site or for the OOTC.

The OOTC view is that sites need to create their own site object technology support groups that function as a mini-OOTC, tailoring OOTC offerings to site-specific needs. The goal has been to have enough successful OOTC-assisted projects at a site, that a skilled practitioner would emerge who could carry on the technology insertion work at a local level.

To further encourage this to happen, the OOTC now has an apprentice program in place to facilitate identification of a promising candidate (usually one who has the knowledge and the drive necessary to be a leader), negotiate with site management to get support for the candidate providing object-oriented mentoring services at the local level, and then work closely with the candidate to teach them technology insertion through actual practice.

Five apprentices have been graduated by the OOTC and are successfully delivering mentoring services at their sites.

Cross-IBM information exchange

Another important aspect of a corporate technology center is that it is approached by numerous groups with similar interests or problems. The center is well positioned to serve as a sort of object-technology matchmaker, pointing projects to other folks who may have already struggled with and solved similar concerns.

To enhance the ability to do this, the OOTC created an object-oriented project survey that was circulated throughout the company. The survey was aimed at capturing a high-level set of information on as many OO projects as possible. This information included type of project, importance of project to the business, platforms used and targeted, languages, libraries, and tools used, productivity and quality results, and ratings of the success of the use of object technology. The survey received a good response, and provided a very good repository from which to understand the scope of IBM's use of the technology, and answered questions about whether someone has used a particular tool or tried a particular approach to using object technology.

Support of IBM strategies

As stated earlier, the OOTC is not a strategy group in that it is not directly responsible for determining an overall IBM strategy for the creation of object enabling products. Two purposes related to strategies are, however, served by the OOTC.

First, the OOTC reviews and comments on various product plans and directions by bringing to bear the group's understanding of what is needed by object technology practitioners in the way of object technology enabling products.

Second, an understanding of emerging products and strategies by OOTC members is needed in order to help mentoring customers make informed decisions on object technology enablers and on the likely directions that their products will need to take in the future.

Support of research

The OOTC is not a research group, but it has maintained contact with IBM research activities to some degree in order to understand what tools or techniques may be emerging.

The OOTC has also participated in some research with the Consortium for Management of Emerging Software Technologies (Comsoft) in the area of object-oriented metrics and object-oriented testing. This was a valuable way of gaining knowledge in areas where OOTC members did not have a lot of experience or a lot of internal information to draw on. This research produced some handbooks on metrics and testing that have been used as reference material in continuing OOTC efforts on these topics.

Publicity of object technology

The body of OOTC offerings and activities has a very important side benefit. From pitches to managers and technical people, to announcements in forums about OOTC offerings, to supporting site object-technology information days, to conferences, the range of activities serves to put object technology in the public eye. This is a key function of a technology center. It is often this easy access to useful information that provides the impetus for an individual or a project to make the commitment to investigate and utilize a technology.

Summary of activities

A workshop on Corporate Object Technology Centers was held at the 1993 Object Oriented Programming, Systems, Languages, and Applications (OOPSLA) conference. That workshop produced a list of possible roles for an object technology center (OTC). Table 2.1 below compares the services that the

OOTC provides with the list of roles generated at the OOPSLA workshops.

The entries in the table are defined as follows:

- P—a primary OOTC activity

- S—a secondary OOTC activity

- N—not an OOTC activity

Table 2.1   Comparison of OOTC activities and OOPSLA list

OOPSLA-defined OTC activities	OOTC focus
Education/knowledge broker	P
Build book library	S
Newsletters	S
Seminars	S
Mentoring	P
Support pilot projects	P
Apprenticeships	P
Object-oriented hot line	P
Customizing technology for projects	P
Monitoring project status	S
Drive cross-project information	P
Infrastructure for cross-project use	S
Change organizational culture	P
Reuse management	S
Manage vendor relationships	N
Coordinate training	N
Tool acquisition and licensing	N
Tool evaluation	S
Ensure unified view from consultants	N
Business strategy synchronization	N
Evaluate class libraries	P
Justify object technology center	P
Build common view of architecture	N
Contribute to state-of-the-art	S
Develop custom methods	P
Develop reusable frameworks	N

Table 2.1 Comparison of OOTC activities and OOPSLA list (continued)

OOPSLA-defined OTC activities	OOTC focus
Develop handbooks	P
Coding guidelines	P
Reuse guidelines	P
Management presentations	P
Promote company activities externally	S
Lobby for support of technology	P

Lessons learned in the evolution of the OOTC

The OOTC has had evolution built into its plans since the beginning. This does not imply that the path of evolution was known, but only that it was understood that evolution was a necessary component of becoming and remaining an effective technology insertion force in the company. The OOTC operating policies ensured evolution of the group by forcing it to:

- add new staff with skills that filled gaps in the OOTC knowledge base, particularly in emerging areas of the technology

- monitor and react to changing requirements for services from the OOTC customer set

- solicit and react to evaluations of OOTC services to ensure that the services are as useful as possible

- keep consultants current by working with projects and helping them to apply the technology to real problems

Looking back over the four years of its existence, it is easy to see that the OOTC has evolved in some very real ways, some of which were described in more detail in earlier sections. Some of the lessons learned and the evolutionary steps that those lessons have driven are detailed in the following subsections.

Customers want strong recommendations

Customers want the OOTC to be able to definitively make strong recommendations on such things as methods, process, and tools in order to save them time on investigations and trial and error usage.

The OOTC evolution toward being able to accomplish that has really been driven by increased experience. While there were people experienced with application of the technology on the staff when the OOTC was formed, these people had no real experience as technology-insertion/mentoring professionals. This probably tempered OOTC recommendations and perhaps even made them slightly weak. But consequent consulting experiences have provided very practical experiences working with numerous different methods, tools, languages, and process approaches and have provided the background necessary for strong recommendations on what works best in particular situations.

These experiences have manifested themselves most in documents, such as the methods evaluations document where stronger criteria for choosing a method and weighing different methods against those criteria is made, and in the development of *The OOTC Workbook-Driven Approach to OO Software Development* document which is directly based on OOTC mentoring practice.

The OOTC consulting practice has also evolved toward being able to provide rules of thumb that apply to the various phases of the development life cycle, again, with these rules being derived from experience.

Consultants must leave knowledge behind

The mentoring provided early on was fairly ad hoc and unstructured, based mainly on the knowledge contained in the consultant's head. This was beneficial, but with more and more complex consulting engagements it became clear that documentation of what was being advocated was needed. That is, if the OOTC was going to make recommendations or propose rules of thumb on approaches to analysis, design, implementation, etc., it had to be able to leave something behind that enabled the clients to revisit what had been said after the OOTC team had left the site.

This has driven work to create *The OOTC Workbook-Driven Approach to OO Software Development* document as a kind of paper consultant. It allows clients (or non-clients) to read and understand particular work products and particular approaches to developing those work products.

C++ coding conventions and class library development documents have also been created to capture recommendations for the design and implementation cycle.

Work products are more important than techniques

In the industry, in IBM, and in the OOTC, the debate over the perfect method and notation has raged. Even within the OOTC, the consultants have not been able to reach agreement on one approach. As OOTC consultants worked more and more with each other and as they assessed the varying approaches that they each had to modeling, analysis, and design, it became clear that the only opportunity for a true consensus was on the *content*, not the form, of work products that were produced at each step of the development life cycle.

This has led to focus on crisp and detailed descriptions of the work products that should be produced while offering a variety of techniques (with pros and cons listed) that could be used to derive those work products. OOTC mentors use these guidelines to recommend templates for project workbooks. Workbooks are collections of the important work products resulting from each phase of the development process. These work product guidelines have been documented in detail in *The OOTC Workbook-Driven Approach to OO Software Development* document which is directly based on OOTC mentoring practice.

For example, in the two approaches to object-oriented development discussed earlier, both assume the development of analysis, design and code workbooks that adhere to the same set of information content guidelines. This work product focus makes the most sense, because after all, the workbooks will remain long after the mentors have left. Another benefit is that a new mentor can come on board and pick up quickly by starting with the work products that have been developed to date and using his or her own techniques to continue from there.

Site leadership is critical

A central technology group can, without a doubt, provide value. But experience suggests that where the technology will really make an impact across a broader spectrum, versus just a small project, is in those cases where some technical or management person (or better yet, both) takes responsibility for committing the site to the technology and developing detailed plans for infusing the technology at the site.

Our activities have evolved to address this lesson through the creation of the apprentice program, through more participation in site information days to spread the positive word, and through pitches targeted at management stressing the why and how of the move to object technology.

Technology lessons

As stated in the mentoring section, the experience gained while working with a project provides a means to evolve the approach to technology insertion, but it also causes the mentor's understanding of the technology to change. Experience can even drive mentors to evolve the technology itself. For example, the OOTC has moved from a focus on analysis modeling to a use case-driven approach over the years. Experience with the current notations for capturing object interactions has caused the OOTC mentors to slightly modify the various notations to capture additional information critical to the success of the project. The key principle is that OOTC technology evolutions stem from actual need, rather than pure theoretical invention.

The OOTC tends to treat object-oriented work products like objects too, allowing them to iterate, just like one would expect that a project team's object model will change over time. The beauty of an object-oriented approach is that it can support these kinds of changes with minimal impact on the remainder of the system.

Conclusions

An object technology center can be successful if it:

- stays true to the notion of inserting technology through hands-on help from practitioners to real projects

- stays current with the technology as it evolves

- adjusts its offerings as real experience and customer demands dictate

- realizes that its role is to create expert practitioners throughout the company, not to create a consulting business

The increasing number of requests for mentoring services, the demand for documents and conferences, and most importantly, the increased number of object technology projects in the corporation leads the OOTC to feel quite successful in furthering the infusion of the technology in IBM.

The OOTC plans to continue to try to maximize the use of object technology within IBM and to be the most valuable resource an IBM project can have when utilizing object technology.

Future plans are, on the surface, as they have been in the past:

- continue to grow in staff, both in size and in breadth and depth of knowledge

- continue to improve and increase document offerings

- continue to improve consulting skills and approach

- increase emphasis on developing site apprentices

- keep pace with the evolving technology

chapter 3

GSF Object Center, BNR Ltd.

GERARD MESZAROS

Background and introduction

BNR and Northern Telecom

Northern Telecom (NT) is a leading supplier of digital tele-communication equipment. Bell Northern Research (BNR) is its research and development subsidiary. As such, BNR develops the hardware and software for most of NT's products, including the central office telephone exchange known as DMS-100. Telephone exchanges, also known as *switches*, are very large, specialized, embedded real-time systems. They are typically built by teams of developers numbering in the hundreds, and their sizes are measured in millions of lines of code.

The DMS-100F family of systems comprises eight major products, ranging from a local access telephone switch to a signal transfer point. It is implemented in Protel, an advanced highly modular object-based Pascal-like language which most closely resembles Modula-2.

About the Generic Service Framework project

DMS-100 is a family of highly featured telephone switching products delivered to North American and global markets. Each market has specific requirements for a multitude of services (e.g., call waiting, 3-way calling, etc.). These requirements vary from market to market requiring extensive customization or parallel implementations. The Generic Services Framework (GSF) project was launched to establish the leadership in switching software architecture needed for rapid delivery of Northern Telecom's customers' requirements. In response to the changing business needs, the decision was made to redesign the call processing software using object technology to enable faster delivery to global markets of the many variations of services.

Why object technology?

Object technology was chosen because it presented a tangible solution to managing the complexity of large systems. The "divide and conquer" approach was already in use at BNR, but what we lacked was a consistent way to describe the designs. In object technology (OT), we found the terminology and notations to fill in this gap. Much of the DMS-100 system was already "object based." It used frameworks that invoked applications (via records containing procedure variables) as the strategy to develop telephone services quickly and without continually reinventing the basic concept of how call processing was done.

The Protel language has supported inheritance of data (fields in records) since the late 1970s. As part of the GSF project, Protel has been further enhanced to support true (single) inheritance, including classes and objects, as well as public and private methods. The enhanced language is known as Protel-2.

Before the object center

The initial plan to move the development teams to object technology was to "just do it" by seeding the development teams with a few people who had been involved in the pilot project which had successfully used object technology (OT). As the team was increased in size from tens to hundreds, it quickly became apparent that the processes that had been used on the small pilot project (about 20 people) were inadequate to deal with an organization that was an order of magnitude larger. Complicating the issue further was the large degree of parallelism between the development of the GSF framework and the initial applications. This required a much more detailed and rigorous process than was needed for the pilot projects.

The team tasked with developing the framework found it to be too much work to develop both the product and the processes simultaneously. As a result, we decided that we really needed to have a dedicated group that would develop the processes and make them available for all the developers.

Organization and staffing

Establishing the mandate

The mandate of the group was established by a set of interested parties who would become the customers of the object center. The mandate was conceived during a series of meetings attended by these people and the author, assisted by Tim Korson of Software Architects. During these meetings, we brainstormed the kinds of activities we felt the object center needed to undertake to solve our technology insertion problem. We formed a board of directors to represent the customers and created the positions of object center manager and object technology specialist. We also defined a steering committee whose job was to assist the object center manager on a more regular basis. See Figure 3.1. (The board of directors consisted of mostly middle managers, while the steering committee was primarily first-level managers and senior designers with object-oriented experience.)

Note that the GSF Object Center (OC) is not a true corporate object center since it only serves GSF at this time, but since GSF is larger than most other companies, the comparison is appropriate. In the long run, it is anticipated that the OC's mandate will be expanded to cover the whole company.

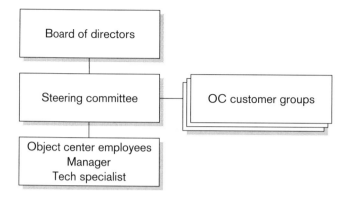

Figure 3.1 Object center organization

The original mandate of the object center could be paraphrased as "acquire, refine and 'productize' the processes and tools necessary for large scale use of object technology within the project and deliver them to the development groups in the form of documentation, templates and training."

A large list of potential activities was generated and prioritized, and the required skill sets were identified. Tim Korson helped us generate this list by asking us questions about the kinds of activities the project expected to do, and what kinds of support the OC would need to provide. This list is reproduced in the Mission section.

Obtaining funding

The creation of a new support group such as an object center requires significant justification to upper management because it is viewed as overhead—it does not contribute directly to the bottom line of the company. The framework and application team managers all felt they required support from an object center to achieve their objectives and pledged to provide the initial staff for the center.

It was felt that it would be easier to secure further funding, if required, once the OC had produced a few useful products. The initial proposal for the OC requested funding for two dedicated people with OOT experience augmented with experienced non-OOT developers from the development groups on 3–6 month rotations. This ensured that the OC would have enough staff to get real work done, and the rotated people would gain valuable experience they could take back to their group. Another objective this helped satisfy was to make the OC very responsive to its customers (to keep it from being perceived as an ivory tower.)

The proposal was submitted to the management team, starting with the managers representing the framework and applications teams to get confirmation of their contributions. This willingness of the customers to contribute people was a key factor in getting upper management acceptance of the proposal. The other key selling point of the proposal was the reduction of the technology risk of the project. Since OT was still fairly new, we could not find off-the-shelf methodologies and training for all aspects of the project. The argument that we needed a group to take the best available information and synthesize it into a suitable set of handbooks was readily accepted by senior management.

The final decision to be made was where the OC should be located in the organization. The two leading contenders were the existing process and tools group or as part of our development organization. It was decided that we needed to maximize the organizational learning by creating a very close partnership between the OC and its clients, the framework and application groups. It was felt that this could be best accomplished by making the OC part of the development team, leaving the move of the OC into the process and tools group for when we were mature enough to spread the gospel beyond the GSF team.

Initial staffing

The senior technology specialist was quickly hired to form the nucleus of the OC from a technical point of view. One of our framework managers agreed to manage the group part time until a full-time manager could be found. Several, though not all, of the promised rotational people were named; the OC was up and running! An issue we ran into very early on was deciding upon the top priority item. There was so much to be done! (It's like opening a Pandora's box; while you are still naive, you can't imagine all the things you haven't realized that you really need.)

Early results

We struggled through the first three months, trying to make tangible progress at defining a methodology for the team to use, as well as defining the criteria for selecting a CASE tool to support it. Meanwhile, the design teams were going full tilt defining the architecture and began asking how they should be documenting the design. The OC had to quickly produce templates for the analysis and design work products the design teams were producing. This was done jointly with the architecture team, whose task was to review all the team designs to ensure that they could be integrated into a single working system. It was the need to review the work products that really drove home the need for common document formats and content. Unfortunately, the templates could only be given to the design teams four weeks before they were to give the completed documents to the architecture team, and this caused some teams to have to do a lot of rework. We kept referring to this as "not quite in time process definition." At one point, the OC was using the bulk of the architecture team and all of the prototyping team's resources to help define the first cut at the process and work-products.

Part of the purpose for defining a process for the design teams to use was to dramatically increase the focus on up-front design. In the telecommunications industry, we deal with a large number of similar requirements from different customers. This has resulted in much similar software being developed over the years. A key step in the process we wanted to define was to do requirements compression by abstracting customer specific requirements into more generic ones that encompassed all the various requirements (though at less detail). We deliberately decided to over-emphasize this by defining a process which put more emphasis on requirements gathering and abstraction before getting into the design and coding phase. (Later, as the team became more experienced in executing this waterfall-like process, we introduced the concept of iteration and incremental development.)

Use cases (from Jacobson) were introduced as a means to capture requirements. This resulted in thousands of use cases which were very hard to manage. The designers also found this very frustrating because most of their self-esteem had previously come from coding. Because all the requirements and analysis work was being captured in documents, many designers felt it was not design work.[*]As we became more familiar with the techniques, we learned to write more abstract use cases, which significantly improved their usefulness and reduced their number by an order of magnitude resulting in a simpler (though still non-trivial) use-case management problem.

_____

* "If it's not in code, it can't be a real design!" In retrospect, a CASE tool might have helped by making the designers feel like they were doing more than just writing documents.

Mission of the object center

The mandate of the object center (its reason for existence) is to put in place the infrastructures (processes, tools, methodologies, mentoring, etc.) to allow large-scale adoption of object technology within GSF.

The original mandate and activities of the OC were:

- concentrate on high-leverage activities to free up the time of key resources[*] and to derisk the program; use external resources wherever possible. Specific deliverables and activities are:

  – handbooks for design and test processes, methodologies and notations

  – handbooks for management (progress metrics, milestone planning, design complexity metrics)

  – provide technical consulting on domain analysis and design

  – provide management consulting to managers of object-oriented projects

  – fund research into high risk areas

  – coordinate tools evaluation and development efforts

  – provide list of consultants-for-hire to managers

  – provide technology and management training

Activities of the object center

Table 3.1 lists the activities and defines priorities as

- P—primary activity

- S—secondary activity

- N—not an activity of the object center

---

[*] …the few experienced people we had who had acquired object knowledge on the pilot project.

Table 3.1 Object center activities

Activity	Priority
Education/knowledge broker	P
Build book library	N
Newsletters	S
Seminars	S
Mentoring	S
Support pilot projects	S
Apprenticeships	N
Object-oriented hot line	S
Customizing technology for projects	N
Monitoring project status	N
Drive cross-project information	S
Infrastructure for cross-project use	S
Change organizational culture	S
Reuse management	N
Manage vendor relationships	S
Tool acquisition and licensing	P
Tool evaluation	P
Ensure unified view from consultants	S
Business strategy synchronization	N
Evaluate class libraries	N
Justify object technology center	S
Build common view of architecture	N
Contribute to state-of-the-art	S
Develop custom methods	P
Develop reusable frameworks	N
Develop handbooks	P
Coding guidelines	S
Reuse guidelines	P
Management presentations	S
Promote company activities externally	S
Lobby for support of technology	N

CHAPTER 3: GSF OBJECT CENTER, BNR LTD.

Education & information broker

Book libraries   Most departments within GSF have their own book libraries. The object center does keep a list of suggested reading for project teams new to GSF and object technology.

Newsletters and seminars   The object center runs a series of lunch-time learning sessions on a variety of topics related to object technology and the GSF project.

Training programs   The OC has developed a number of training courses in object technology. Several courses were developed specifically for us by outside vendors and others have been used unchanged. Since BNR operates at many sites spread across several different countries, we have developed working relationships with several alternative training vendors. The basic OT training curriculum includes:

- two-day "Introduction to OT" (vendor A)

- three days of "OO Analysis and Design Training" (vendor A)

or

- five-day "OO Analysis and Design Training" (vendor B)

followed by one or more of:

- five-day "OO Case Studies" course (vendor B)

- five-day "OO Design and Programming Idioms" (vendor C)

- two-day "Managing OO Projects" course (vendor B)

There are several recommended training tracks through these courses. Most design staff will take the two vendor A courses or the vendor B course for their initial training. They would follow up with either the vendor B "Case Studies" course, or the vendor C "Idioms" course. Most managers would take the "Managing OO Projects" course only.

The OC also provides training specific to the project, specifically:

- "GSF Overview"
- "GSF Architecture"
- "GSF Development Process"

In addition, the OC evaluates other courses for possible use within BNR and GSF. Specific examples include:

- "Introduction to Patterns"
- "Writing Patterns"
- "Testing OO Software"

The OC works with the BNR/NT training center by subcontracting much of the logistical work, (registration, classrooms, purchase orders, etc.) but retains ownership of the technical content of the courses. All course participants are asked to fill out an evaluation form; this feedback is used to evolve the courses to meet the changing needs of the design community. Additionally, on pilot runnings of new courses, evaluation forms are filled out for each major section of the course, and a debriefing session is held at the end of the course to collect additional feedback.

Object-oriented hot line   The OC has set up a "news group" about object technology where people can exchange information.

Consulting and mentoring

The object center has been heavily involved in providing mentoring to the application and framework teams on how to apply object technology. We had originally hoped to build up a pool of object-oriented mentors which we could loan out to whoever needed them but we have had trouble building up such a pool. (Anyone who knows how to apply the stuff is even more valuable to us in defining and capturing our processes!) As a result, most of the pure object-oriented (as opposed to architecture usage) mentoring has been achieved by hiring consultants whom we make available to the teams on demand.

Managing consultants   The OC acted as a clearing house for requests for consultants, matching up available consultants with requests for help. Initially, we found considerable resistance to using outside people, but as these consultants have become more experienced in our problem domain, both their usefulness and acceptance has increased considerably.

We tried conducting design reviews with external consultants but found this to be very frustrating as we never had suitable documentation for them to review, and the external consultants did not have enough problem domain knowledge to understand what documentation we did have. We now realize that you have to view your consultants as a longer term investment. This involves giving them the same kind of problem domain training as you would any full-time employee and giving them the time to come up to speed on your domain.

Apprenticeships   We have rotated a number of people through the object center as a way of getting people more familiar with the concepts of object technology. This was also done to keep the OC closely connected with the real problems faced by the development teams. As the OC does not do any actual development, it cannot actually provide true apprenticeships.

Change organizational culture

The OC has been heavily involved in changing the culture of the design organization. A key component of this has been an advocacy role of championing concepts such as design traceability and design for testability. It has also played a key role in improving the process maturity of the organization.

Process maturity assessment We have recently conducted a Trillium assessment of the GSF organization and the object center is priming the continuous improvement programs to move us to level 4 maturity.[*] The OC is leading the initiative by assisting teams in the capture and improvement of their processes. As part of this activity, the OC is providing tools to track problems in the software or processes and to track corrective actions identified through software review processes such as design reviews and code inspections.

Tool evaluation & acquisition

Tools evaluations One of the tasks of the OC since day one has been to select and deploy a computer-aided software engineering (CASE) tool for capturing our designs. We had tried to capture some designs in various CASE tools, but found them all lacking for a system the size of ours. Most worked on a small scale, but none could really explain a design to the viewer without an expert narrator being present. As a result, we held off on our CASE tool buying decision for over a year until we had developed a realistic vision of what we wanted it to do based on some real experience. We ended up using mostly SDL capture tools as part of the requirements gathering process and OMTool (Version 1, now discontinued) to capture our domain and analysis models where these became too large to easily capture using FrameMaker.

Tools acquisition The OC is in charge of all major tool acquisitions for the organization. After a tool is selected, it will assess the number of licenses required, establish the

---

[*] Trillium is a Bell Canada and Northern Telecom defined software maturity model combining aspects of both SEI and ISO software and management maturity models. The level numbers are very similar in meaning to the SEI levels.

budgets and projected payback, and negotiate with the vendors for group or site licences. Many of our tools need to be used by every designer, but for short periods of the design cycle. We have tried to obtain *floating licenses* (*n* simultaneous usages) for these tools to keep the costs manageable.

Custom tool development   Our idea of what a CASE tool should do for us has evolved significantly since we wrote up the first requirements specification for it early in the life of the OC. We have learned that different types of users need tools that do different things. For example, our framework developers want a basic Rumbaugh notation modeling tool with which to capture their analysis models and designs. The users of the framework want something which will help them create designs that make effective use of the framework.

We believe that the more specialized a CASE tool is, the more it can do for you, especially in the area of providing guidance. It is worth asking yourself, before making a tool buying decision, what you expect the tool to do beyond drawing diagrams. If the answer is "not much," you should re-evaluate the cost (both monetary and time) of adopting a CASE tool versus the expected benefit.

Custom method development

Requirements capture & modelling methodology   We are defining the methodology for capturing the requirements of each of our applications on the framework. This involves recording all requests for framework support (RFS) in a database and linking them to the description of how this RFS can be satisfied with either existing or new framework capabilities. These are being captured in a form very similar to usage patterns; that is, recipes for how to do certain things using the framework. We believe that this will be a very important form of documentation of the framework for our application designers.

We are also looking at other available tools for capturing the requirements for our applications (based on specs given to us by our customers.) So far, we have not found anything that we want to use that will give us more capability or be easier to use than our RFS database.

Design methodology definition   A large part of the work of the object center to date has been in defining a generic object-oriented development methodology. Initially, we were using this as a way to push object-oriented knowledge into the design groups by providing a selected and condensed subset of the information available in external literature captured in a single document known as the *GSF Object-Oriented Design* (*GOOD*) book. We also defined the type of work that should be done in each of a number of iterations and the work products that should be available at each iteration. This was done to provide both managers and designers with an idea of how to spend their time at various points in the project.

In parallel with this activity, the Service Architecture Team (SAT) set out to define a design methodology specifically for designers of telephone services.[*] As this "Service Design Guide" (SDG) has matured, it has become more apparent that the *GOOD* book should be the generalization of the specialized design methodologies, of which the SDG is simply the first. The *GOOD* book will be used as the "default methodology" that all projects will use and specialize as they get more experienced at applying OO to their problem domains.

Test and integration methodology definition   In the area of testing, we have done quite a bit of work on defining a testing methodology. This has been done in conjunction with outside consultants and our framework and application clients. The methodology we have defined includes extensive use of object test harnesses and stubs to allow classes to be tested

---

[*] ...as opposed to designers of the framework itself, or the non-call processing part of the telephone switch. Examples of services include call waiting, call forwarding, and three-way calling.

before large-scale integration. This results in much quicker integration as well as much higher quality software which is more easily retested after any changes are made to it.

Process handbooks

Project management processes definition   Our initial attempt at a project management methodology was to divide the project into Iterations A through F and tell people what percentage of their time they should be spending on requirements capture, domain modeling, analysis modeling, design, implementation, testing, and integration in each of the phases. This was a somewhat waterfall-like approach but we did it to overcome the normal tendency to dive right into detailed design while collecting requirements. Now that the people on the project have had some experience collecting requirements and abstracting them into domain models, we are moving to a more incremental approach. We have defined a number of incremental releases of the project, the first two of which are called Lab 1 and Lab 2 because they are not intended for external use. The framework functionality in each release is driven by the specific functionality that our application groups have committed to support in that release.

For our first lab release, the management team had to be very innovative to reduce the high degree of schedule dependency caused by the fragmentation of functionality into objects. It was very common to be able to reduce an initial schedule that stretched out for more than a year into a third of that time by defining incremental milestones based on a subset of the functionality to be provided with the release. To make it easier to align what would be provided in all the classes, we chose a small number of use cases that would form the focus of the integration efforts. Lab 1 had three macro[*]

---

[*] *Macro increment* is being used to distinguish sub-releases from per-component increments.

increments; the first contained low-level functionality to allocate and destroy objects; the second contained some higher level functionality, while the third and last increment included the first telephone call built on the framework. A key to making this process work was the development of the testing methodology described earlier.

The management practices of Lab 1 have since been further refined as part of the Lab 2 planning exercise and a series of project management workshops. The results were captured in a *Project Management Guide*.

Software agreements   One of the things we found we needed to do was to capture who was going to do what. The design teams became very good at identifying things in common with what other groups were developing, and we often reacted by designating one of the teams as prime on building a particular reusable piece. But this introduced dependencies between parts of the project that may not have previously existed. Sometimes these reusable entities took on lives of their own, looking for broader mandates, etc.. We needed to capture exactly what the group was going to provide and when it would be available.

We introduced the concept of software agreements (SA) to capture this information. The SA captures what functionality will be provided in which iteration (and by what dates). Typically, success paths for basic use cases are the first things covered, followed by more complex use cases and finishing off with the error paths. The *what* is described in the class specification (which becomes part of the long term design documentation), while the *when* becomes part of the project plan.

Coding guidelines and best practices   The OC has developed a set of coding guidelines. These are constantly being refined by examining the best practices seen on the project. Information collected from across the organization is sifted, and the best-in-class examples are published in the best practices handbook. This is an important mechanism for improving the OO programing knowledge of the average designer.

Reuse guidelines

It is very easy to over-stress the concept of code reuse. There is a definite cost associated in making code reusable. Beyond the obvious certification costs, reusable components take longer to design and are typically more expensive in both memory and processor usage. (A classic computer science trade-off, in that one reduces the amount of storage used for the program at the cost of increased cost at run-time in both object instances and method calls.) You need to define how important reuse is to achieving your goals; reuse should not be a goal in its own right.

We have since started to look at what support will be required for reuse. Our architecture and processes have largely shielded us from needing to address this earlier since we use inheritance primarily to define common interfaces (via abstract classes) rather than for implementation (code reuse). We get significant reuse of design and black box use of components from our extensive use of frameworks.

Code reuse   Each of the framework teams has been documenting the interfaces to the objects that they are building. The applications teams will then use these interfaces within their software designs. The implementation of these interfaces are typically provided by different application teams (from those that need to use the interfaces; it is this decoupling of different types of applications that was a major goal of the framework).

The RFS database will form a key part of our reuse database in that it will capture how to use the framework and its classes to build applications.

Design reuse   The other form of reuse that we are pursuing aggressively is design reuse. We are using design patterns as the means for describing and documenting designs which can be applied in many implementations. These have allowed us to move our design discussions farther from the code by providing a more concise vocabulary for describing designs and design issues.

One technique we've found very useful is called *designing for change*; we try to define all the things that may need to be changed in the future (based on our business plans) and decouple them from the parts from which they should be independent. The Strategy Pattern,[1] which involves *objectifying* algorithms, is a good example of how to do this.

Separate from the OC, a team of service design architects was formed to understand how best to design services using the framework and to design a specialized process complete with domain specific versions of requirements and domain and analysis models. This process has been fine-tuned through pilots with the service design groups, and as it matures, it is being captured in a series of design patterns (a *pattern language* for designing telephony services). These patterns are, in turn, being incorporated into a knowledge-based service design tool built on top of the generic object-oriented CASE tool that we purchased for the framework teams. The tool guides service designers through the requirements, domain, analysis, and design phases of the process and generates much of the final executable code for them. The OC's involvement with this activity has centered around providing support for the development of the pattern language as a key knowledge and design reuse enabler.

Justify object center

The existence of a support organization such as an object center needs constant justification. An early form of this activity is the argument for its creation. This should not be considered a primary role, but it cannot be neglected.

Management presentations   On occasion, the OC is called upon to present information about the benefits of object technology to senior management or customers. A standard package is kept up to date so this can be done at short notice.

Promote company activities externally   It isn't an explicit goal of the OC to promote the company per se, but maintaining a high profile in the software development community can improve the caliber of candidates who apply for jobs at your company. (A reputation as a state-of-the-art software development company can't hurt.)

The GFS Object Center has coordinated participation at conferences such as OOPSLA, Object World, Object Expo and Pattern Languages of Programs (PLoP). Members of the GSF team have presented papers at OOPSLA and PLoP and have participated in or organized many workshops at OOPSLA over the past four years.

Evolution of the object center

Mandate evolution

Since its launch, the OC has grown significantly. It has taken on a number of additional roles, including ISO 9000 certification, Trillium (SEI) maturity assessment, and process improvement primeship. It has also added reuse management to its list of activities.

Process ownership evolution

Within our North Carolina lab, the customers of the OC formed a group called the Process Review Board (PRB) consisting primarily of designers. The theory was that since they would have to use the process, they should have a say in defining it. All changes to the process (primarily the GOOD book) had to be sanctioned by the PRB. This ensured a great deal of participation, but resulted in making it difficult to get changes since a lot of people had to be convinced.

The ownership of the process has now been moved from the users of the process (represented by the PRB) to the owners of each project. Each project manager must declare what processes they will use on their project. The creation and documentation of any new processes they require is part of their project plan which must be available before they get the go-ahead for full-scale development. By giving each manager the authority to define their own processes, we avoided the one-size-fits-all problem. A number of processes and process elements are available for reuse, including the *GOOD* book, which has been repositioned as a starter set from which they can pick and choose those elements which are relevant to their project.

Several project managers working on similar problem domains may band together to create a joint process. (A good example of this is the process created for all teams doing telephone service design.)

One problem this approach can create is that groups resistant to change may decide not to use well defined processes. This will be countered by having a true process review board which will have the authority to allow or prevent a project from preceding to full-scale development based on the ability of the processes to meet minimum standards. This is also required for Trillium (and SEI) maturity improvement.

Structure evolution

The structure of the object center has also changed. Initially, the object center reported to the board of directors which had high-level (middle management) representation from each of the key clients. The operations committee consisted of first level managers (or their representatives) and met weekly to review progress of the OC and to direct its efforts. Unfortunately, this group found it hard to ensure a quorum due to lack of time. Much of the day-to-day feedback for the OC came via word of mouth or through the Process Review Board.

OC is now a multisite organization with a single middle-manager in charge of all operations. First level managers at each site report to the OC manager. The notion of a steering committee has been abandoned, with the OC manager getting feedback and requirements from his or her client peers at regular project meetings.

Lessons learned

Use the OC as the focus of your organizational learning

The OC has an important role to play as the focal point of your organization's learning. As such, it must be close to its customers, both geographically and organizationally. This allows the OC to participate in the learning process and record the results for later usage elsewhere in the organization.

Size your effort properly

There is a lot more work to adopting object technology (OT) in a large organization than one might initially imagine. A lot of things you take for granted have to be revisited. To get the full benefit of OT, you will probably have to change a lot more than you might expect at first examination.

Get high-level corporate commitment

It's important to the success of OT insertion that management be committed to its success. One way of ensuring that upper management stays interested and provides the necessary support is to apply OT to a mission-critical project. This makes it very hard for them to ignore and ensures that the right level of investment is made in inserting OT.

Leverage your existing skill base

It is very important to leverage the skills you already possess (don't throw the baby out with the bath water). The retraining of your existing staff should focus on augmenting those skills in which they are strong with the skills in which they are weak. In our case, this meant augmenting the real-time programming skills of our staff by focusing on abstraction and analysis skills, which then lead to OO programming skills.

Don't rush buying a CASE tool

You need to understand your process before you can automate it. A generic CASE tool will force you to follow the generic methodology it supports. You need to ensure that this will be adequate for your needs. Don't hesitate to buy a few seats to try it out, but don't make a decision until you really understand what you need.

View consultants as an investment

Initially, they will seem to be a net drain on you because you will have to spend a lot of time explaining things to them. They will become more valuable to you as they become more familiar with your problem domain, your organizational culture, and your chosen solution.

Evolve the mandate of the OC

Initially, the mandate was focussed on the introduction of OT into the project. As the project team has matured, its needs have changed from requiring help getting started in OT to becoming more mature in its use. This means the OC has evolved from being OT focused to being focused on process improvement. The mandate has to be updated to avoid a mismatch between customers' expectations and what the OC is actively pursuing.

Don't go overboard looking for reuse

It is very easy to over-stress the concept of reuse. There is a definite cost associated in making things reusable. Beyond the obvious certification costs, reusable components take longer to design and are typically more expensive in both memory and processor usage. You need to define how important reuse is to achieving your goals; reuse should not be a goal in its own right. The type of reuse is also important; reuse of analysis results and designs can be of more value than reuse of code. Patterns are a good way to capture the knowledge of your key people for reuse by the whole team.

Conclusions

Making the transition to object technology in a large corporation to address the changing business climate and increasing demands of customers requires considerable commitment. A key component of this commitment is the investment made in an object center. This investment is required because people cannot be expected to learn to develop software using object technology and to develop the required processes at the same time. It is important that OT insertion be driven from within the development organization rather than by a technology group. It is essential that the object center make continuous and visible efforts to stay in touch with its customers at all organizational levels. An object center is also crucial to advancing the process maturity of the organization (as measured by the SEI software maturity model or ISO-9000).

References

1   Erich Gamma, Richard Helm, Ralph Johnson, and John Vlissides,
Design Patterns: Elements of Reusable Object-Oriented Software, Addison-Wesley, 1994.

chapter 4

The Travelers'
Object Systems Center

John Cunningham

Background and introduction

The Travelers Group (TRV) is a diversified financial services firm providing an array of offerings that include investment banking, securities brokerage, asset management, mutual fund management, consumer loans and credit cards, life insurance, annuities, retirement products, health care insurance and administration, commercial property/casualty insurance, personal property, liability, and specialty insurance coverages.

The Travelers' 1993 Annual Report states that the new Travelers Corporation, comprised of the former Primerica and its two 1993 acquisitions, Shearson and Travelers Insurance, had total assets of over $100 billion, total revenues of nearly $7 billion, and net income of almost $1 billion. The insurance operations alone operate with over 25,000 employees in combined home and field office staff.

Most of the insurance services and products referred to above are provided by the Travelers Insurance Group (TIG), which is the collection of operating entities that until January 1994 were independently operated as The Travelers Insurance Companies (TIC). At that time, Primerica Corporation acquired TIC and formed a new corporation that adopted the strong brand name of The Travelers for the entire corporation. The majority of the investment services fall within the Smith Barney Shearson (SBS) organization, of which the Shearson component was also acquired by Primerica in 1993 and is now an operating group of the parent corporation.

Within the Travelers Insurance Group exists a technology core that supports the operational business lines: personal, property casualty claim, asset management and pension services, and managed care and employee benefits. The TIG core group is the distributed environment division (DED) and exists primarily to work with the TIG business lines to develop strategic business solutions that leverage distributed technologies. The four pillars of DED include distributed systems management, distributed operating systems, information products, and distributed architectures.

Why object technology?

Early in 1992, the precursor organization to the distributed architectures group within DED identified object technology (OT) as the most important directional technology that could be brought to bear in developing distributed computing applications. The conclusion was supported by observing that the market leaders in the financial, software, and systems integration industries had committed to extensive adoption of OT. OT is the soul of today's leading software technologies: *objects pervade the most basic elements of the leading distributed computing environments, ranging from operating systems to network services to graphical user interfaces.*

Without a knowledge base of object technologies built from experience, The Travelers could only weakly apply the powerful distributed technologies that were translating into a competitive advantage in the information rich insurance and finance industries. Without a rich infrastructure to support OT, The Travelers would be dependent on third parties to provide expertise, thereby incurring high expense and risking exposure of our business processes to outsiders.

We concluded that creating an object systems center presented The Travelers with the best option to develop institutional OT competence in a cost effective, timely, efficient, and high-quality manner. By early 1993, pockets of object technology were moving forward in the organization, but they were only loosely coupled. This arrangement was inefficient, and delayed and threatened to jeopardize the full benefit that we expected to gain through developing a more comprehensive, unified competence across all business areas. Real object technology competence can only be achieved through experience, therefore it is imperative that each experience build upon another.

The business processing platform

It was clear that adoption of the object systems center concept would have direct implications for systems development, ranging from how, by whom, in what time frame, and with what tools systems are developed. These implications for the systems aspects of Travelers operations must be consistent with the key business objectives. Table 4.1 highlights the core implications for systems development and the key business objectives that our systems support.

Table 4.1   The business processing platform

Business objectives	Systems implications
Innovate new information based products and services in new and existing markets	Shorten cycle times from, project scoping to project delivery
Respond quickly and certainly to market force changes for competitive advantage	Improve system quality and robustness through large scale reuse of existing components
Minimize cost structure for information intensive business operations	Comanage cross-functional development teams with business and technical player/coaches
Offer high quality, targeted products and services	Transform from a systems-development to systems-integration group

The listed business objectives require the types of systems described by the systems implications. When taken together, this combination of business objectives and systems implications represents our business processing platform. Systems cannot exist in a vacuum: they must be motivated and defined by key business objectives. Conversely, in today's competitive, changing, information driven marketplace we must process information in innovative and efficient ways to meet our business objectives. Thus, there is a bond between the business and technology that ultimately determines a firm's profitability and likelihood to continue as a going concern.

In evaluating the performance of our business, we seek to optimize along appropriate dimensions. The three measurements of greatest importance to successful systems operations are reduction of cost, improvement in quality, and shortening of cycle times. The important, but broader, metrics for the businesses are along dimensions of high frequency of innovation, high quality services, and immediacy of responsiveness to customers that translate into greater profitability. There is no one-to-one relationship between the business and technology criteria, since they must all exist in the aggregate to provide the excellence and business leverage for which we strive.

Funding the proposal

We proposed in the summer of 1993 to assemble the ongoing disparate and uncoordinated object technology efforts into a centralized, consolidated, focused area fully committed to object technology: *The Travelers Object Systems Center (OSC)*. Our expectation was that the OSC could provide the kernel around which each interested business area could grow its own competence without redundant investments in time, materials, and personnel. As a critical byproduct of this effort, we would effectively reengineer the systems delivery process within the company.

The core systems area is financed each year through contributions from the profit centers of the company, the business lines. Some of these contributions are mandatory and are driven by cost allocation derived from hardware units, deployed systems, and software in use per business unit. However, in the areas dedicated to new development techniques and research, the contributions are made more voluntarily. The business unit I/S chiefs must buy into the core area's recommendation to pursue a program and then commit to funding some percentage of the effort. Each business unit determines the amount they will contribute as constrained by: (a) funds available, (b) expected value of that program throughout the coming year, and (c) relative use of the program when compared to other business units' expectations. These contributions are then spread out through the year by the core staff charging to business unit.

In the case of the OSC, the charges are handled both ways for different center functions. The OSC members directly contributing to projects charge their time to business unit accounts, while the OSC permanent staff manage their own account and allocate the charges monthly to the business units as per the agreed upon percentages. From the lines of business perspective, they have a known fixed cost throughout the year and a controllable variable cost associated with project initiatives. This creates an incentive to undertake serious projects, so as to maximize the return on the fixed investments. This is a recurring process on a year-by-year basis, although the business units were asked to make a minimum commitment for a three year period to ensure stability and viability of the OSC initiative.

Mission

The OSC exists to support business areas in the development of object technology-based information systems to deliver reengineered business processes or new business ventures at a reduced cost, in shorter time frames, and with high quality. The delivery of these systems includes the creation of an object technology competency in the business area to maintain and enhance the system, and to enable and empower them to embark on subsequent similar efforts independently from the OSC.

Ultimately, the mission of the OSC is to be pared back considerably as the business areas develop breadth and depth of proficiency in these technologies. The OSC is intended as a closed end entity with a reasonable life span of three to five years. Viewing the center as an entity whose purpose is to enhance the context for knowledge acquisition and communication, the main activities are to:

- *leverage* the total corporate investment in object technology

- *expedite* knowledge transfer across the organization

- *facilitate* corporate wide design and code reuse

- *reduce* development costs and cycle times

- *improve* overall quality

Activities

We divide the functions or activities of the OSC into five categories that are all necessary to ensure the success of the endeavor. These areas are (1) operating process, (2) human resources and organization, (3) management process, (4) value system, and (5) technology. It is our contention that most firms that would adopt object technology centers would overemphasize the technology and management areas at the expense of the human resource and operating process areas.

In reviewing our disparate activities through the early adoption of object technology at the Travelers, we concluded that the key ingredient, by far, was the people. Second to the people is the need for an operational framework in which they can interact. The individuals and their interaction experiences within the operational framework provide a fertile environment for the creation, shaping, and propagation of a new value system. The general domain of the technology is fixed, and specific tools and methods adoption are to be selected to fit the value system that has evolved. Similarly, the management style and governance structures should remain organic in nature to afford rapid growth and flexibility.

With these thoughts in mind, the following description of the OSC will be devoted mainly to describing the roles and responsibilities of the OSC members and the process framework in which they operate. The OSC organization is segmented into two logical components: (1) project staff, and (2) support staff. The project staff is the set of individuals who will be assigned to specific projects to create systems and effect technology transfer to the sponsoring business area. The support staff, or *backwall*, performs those roles that cut across projects to provide greater leverage for all. The most tangible benefit to the OSC is the centralization of the backwall functions to eliminate costs due to functional redundancy across business areas.

The operating process: using the object technology center

Utilization of the OSC has two objectives for the line business areas: (1) development of object technology applications, and (2) transfer of object technology skills and knowledge. Additionally, the OSC must achieve two feedback objectives for increasing the Center's value: (1) extracting reusable components, and (2) learning new lessons with each experience to leverage knowledge. Figure 4.1 depicts a process model of how the center operates in support of these objectives.

As shown in the figure below, there are three general phases of employing the OSC. First, interest is stimulated in object technology through internal or external marketing. More desirably, the Travelers' System Design Center recommends that a project under consideration utilize the OSC. The project management team meets with representatives of the OSC to discuss and review the appropriateness of applying OT to the specific project at hand. At this point a go/no-go decision is made. Assuming the parties agree to move forward, the project moves into the OSC to begin the analysis, assessment, and segmentation tasks. From the initial planning

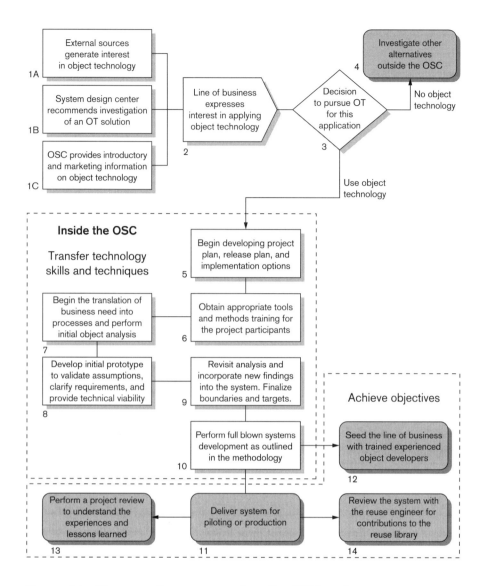

Figure 4.1   The operating process—how the OSC works

and definition, the OSC would undertake the technology and
skills transfer to the project team members from the line of
business. This occurs over the active life of the project, with
the project physically residing in the OSC for at least three
months, so that the business-line systems people have an

object immersion experience. After that period, the project moves back to the business area's site, with at least one OSC staff member supporting the project full time at that site.

The process culminates in a four part conclusion that provides measurable value to both the business area and the OSC. As depicted, the system is delivered and the members of the project team, from the line of business, are now trained and experienced in applying object technology. The OSC now must study the project to mine useful information concerning execution of the plan and potential for generalizing components that were built on the project for the first time.

Subsequent projects in the line business area require less hands-on involvement from the OSC once they get past the early planning and analysis stages. However, the OSC does continue involvement on an as needed basis to ensure consistency and to continue to gather information about the new ventures.

Human resources: the backwall organization

As indicated above, there is a set of individuals who handle the roles of the OSC that are supportive of the individual project teams. In reality, we have been constrained by both available talent and funding and have required these backwall staffers to play active project team roles as well. Below is a detailed description of the key roles, their primary responsibilities, and their degree of authority. Notes are also made concerning the roles' interactions with each other, and the skills that candidates for such positions should have. These roles and their organization are shown in Figure 4.2.

Director of strategic object systems development In general, the director of strategic object systems development is responsible for setting direction and leading the day-to-day activities of the OSC. This includes the following responsibilities:

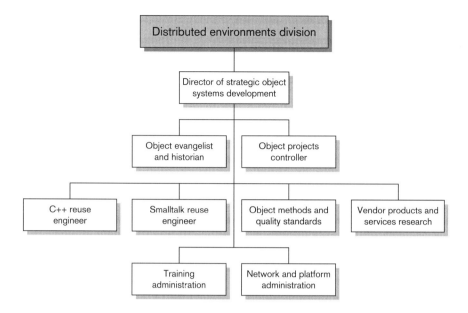

Figure 4.2 The OSC backwall support team

- positioning the resources of the Center to support key business objectives

- maintaining an organizational culture conducive to effective communication, openness, and high-performance development teams, support staff, and management

- ensuring that individuals are empowered with the necessary technical, communication, and business skills to effectively carry out their roles

- determining the appropriateness of key technologies, from a business cost/benefit standpoint as well as a technical merit standpoint

- managing the cost and complexity of the development methodology

The director is primarily accountable for the quality of the product the OSC provides, namely a consistent, cost-effective, leveragable diversity of high-performing applications and application development teams throughout the organization. This is measured by the business lines and systems areas on a project by project basis. The director interacts extensively with the management of the business lines and systems areas to gather feedback, identify development and leadership needs, and evolve and present the strategy for meeting those needs.

The director continually interacts with all individuals filling roles in the OSC to provide leadership and focus toward the goals of the organization, and to be advised of potential problems and opportunities in both products and projects. The object evangelist and historian works closely with the director to seek out opportunities for the OSC to position the service and provide value.

We recommend that the director position be filled by someone who has extensive experience in developing distributed applications, including heavy object-oriented development experience. Leadership, communication, and management skills are used heavily in this position. Most importantly, the individual in this position must have the ability to grasp the needs of the business partner at both the detailed and strategic levels and effectively market and deliver real solutions to meet those business needs.

Object evangelist and historian   The object evangelist and historian is responsible for identifying and obtaining opportunities to provide the services of the OSC to the business lines and systems areas. One key facet of effective project marketing is a thorough understanding of the history of past object-oriented projects. The object evangelist and historian is responsible for maintaining a documented history of all object projects at the Travelers. Ongoing projects should be studied and post-mortems conducted upon completion. This history not only prevents the repetition of mistakes by the organization, but provide a valuable asset in marketing OSC services.

The director of strategic object development is a key partner, since the object evangelist and historian is the agent who carries out the director's positioning of OSC services. The second primary interaction is with the project teams to document and conduct postmortems of object-oriented projects.

This role requires knowledge of the Travelers information systems department (ISD) organization as well as a proven ability to add value to the business lines. The responsibilities of this position require that the individual be able to quickly size up and understand the nature of business problems and strategies in order to correctly market technology solutions and ensure a fit between the solution and the problem.

Object projects controller   The object projects controller supports the director of strategic object systems development by ensuring the quality of each development project at a detailed level. This individual manages the technical player coaches and reviews each project to ensure quality application of methods, design, and project management.

The object projects controller provides assurance to the business customer that the project development effort has the promised quality and cost-effectiveness. The object projects controller is advised by the object methodology and standards promotor as the organizational development methodology evolves. The reuse engineers advise the object projects controller concerning the status of the Travelers reusable resources. The object projects controller ensures that the appropriate levels of reuse are occurring in the development projects.

This role requires technical development expertise, including object-oriented experience. Good management/ leadership skills are required. The management style should not be a strong-handed enforcer approach, but rather a flexible, open leadership style which educates and encourages buy-in to standards and methods.

Reuse engineers, Smalltalk and C++   The reuse engineer is responsible for working with object development player/coaches and class designers from ongoing C++ and Smalltalk development projects to identify opportunities for both reuse of previously developed objects, as well as development of objects reusable in the future.

The primary focus of any development project is to serve the immediate need. It is seldom possible to design and build objects with generic functionality mid-stream in a development project. The role of the reuse engineer is to bring to each project design a perspective broader than the current need, and influence the design where possible. To the extent that generalization is not possible, the reuse engineer revisits potentially valuable objects after project implementation and either develops them into generic objects, or documents a design for a future project to reimplement for reuse.

The reuse engineer is also responsible for researching reuse techniques and technologies, as well as cross-language and cross-platform object technologies (such as Common Object Request Broker Architecture, and System Object Management) and facilitating their use, if appropriate at the Travelers.

The primary interaction is with the project teams, past and present. The vendor products and library researcher is also a valuable partner in identifying which reuse technologies are in their infancy and are expected to be available in the near term.

The reuse engineer must have a thorough understanding of good object-oriented design, construction, and an ability to create generic objects from application-specific objects. Past experience on object-oriented development projects is necessary. This role would work well as a rotating responsibility among the object-oriented development population.

Object methodology and standards promotor (OMSP)   Object-oriented design is a growing discipline. Each development group tends to evolve its own design methodology and rules.

The responsibility of this role is to do so for the Travelers environment. The OMSP is responsible for studying past TIC object-oriented projects and identifying the standards and methodologies which have been used successfully. As there has been no OMSP in the past, each project has been unique. From these a common approach should be synthesized.

Team communication or workgroup tools can have a positive impact on the methodology of the team. As these technologies mature and new products become available, the OMSP should seek them out and assess their potential value for the TIC object-oriented methodology. The primary role of the OMSP is that of an educator to the project teams, rather than an enforcer of rules. There are many ways to effectively structure an object-oriented project, and the goal of standardization should be subordinate to the goal of effectiveness. The OMSP is a consultant to fledgling development projects, but a student of mature projects.

The primary interaction is with the project teams, especially with the player/coaches and the class designers. The OMSP is a resource to these individuals to assist them in structuring the project and educating the rest of the team in object-oriented design principles. The vendor products and library researcher is essential in evolving the methodology as new products become available. Outside education and investigation of vendor relationships and consulting groups is useful in bringing good structure to the Travelers methodology.

The OMSP needs object-oriented development experience to be able to ground theoretical ideas in the context of real project development. The OMSP does not need to be an expert as much as a facilitator and a conduit of principles learned by individuals on multiple projects, both inside and outside of the organization.

Vendor products and library researcher (VPLR)   The primary responsibility of this role is to establish and maintain relationships with vendors of technologies used in object-oriented development at the Travelers. The second key responsibility of the VPLR is vital to the effective support of object-oriented development. The VPLR must keep in close touch with the technical and design issues faced by object-oriented development projects. This interaction is a payoff derived from the co-location of the support team and the project teams, and requires that the VPLR be well-versed in the common needs and real-life issues faced by object-oriented development teams. The VPLR should also actively research tools and libraries available for purchase and evaluate them on a pilot basis in collaboration with the development teams.

The primary alliance/interaction is with developers to understand issues facing development teams, understand practical limitations of development tools, and pilot potential tools and libraries for general use in company projects. The second major interaction is with product vendors, consulting resources, and printed media to identify solutions to problems and effective development tools. Emphasis should be on understanding the capabilities of the tools in the Travelers development environment, as opposed to the technical virtues of features of the products themselves. Products should be rigorously proven in actual development settings before incorporation into a methodology. Interactions with the reuse engineers and the OMSP is vital to effective development, since products can play a large role in determining methodology and facilitating reuse.

This role requires both the ability to support products and projects from a technical perspective, and a first-hand understanding of real-life development issues. Individuals filling this responsibility should have a development background in object-oriented technology, or at least rotate periodically as developers on object-oriented projects.

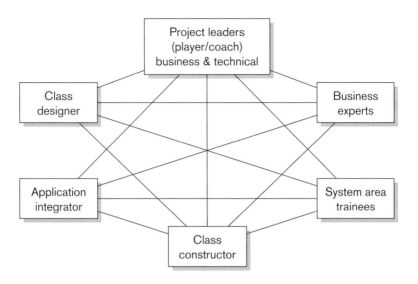

Figure 4.3   The OSC project team structure

Project team structure and dynamics

Figure 4.3 provides a depiction of the operating team structure. While the team has clearly defined leaders, it should be small and flat to provide the greatest degree of communication and knowledge sharing. Please keep in mind that the roles identified in each box do not indicate that there is a one to one correspondence of people to roles. Some players play several roles, while some roles are distributable among several players. The important aspects are to match the project needs with the role allocation and to assign roles to individuals who both are prepared and motivated to excel at them.

   Business application player/coach (BAPC)   Business group members of the development teams need some type of focus for coordinating how business is to be conducted through the program interface. The BAPC is that individual and carries the authority to make changes to the design based on business need, or is in the position to act as the liaison between the focused members of the development team and the business area. The BAPC uses the same design methodology as the object development player/coach below. Responsibilities are to:

- formulate detailed business rules and identify the business process from an event standpoint

- assist the object development player/coach in identifying classes, their behaviors, and interrelations

- create use case and class documentation, describing the possible classes identified from a business perspective

- create user documentation

The BAPC role is a function that is closely tied to the object development player/coach role below. Alliances between the customer business area and the development team are imperative to the success of the individual in this role. Interactions extend outward from this role to all aspects of the project, with direct daily interaction with the development team emphasizing the object development player/coach. The BAPC serves as a filter from the business customer for the development team with emphasis on keeping the object development player/coach informed at all times.

Background: Business with strong technical training. Training: programming language of choice, object design training.

Object development player/coach (ODPC)   This role is the linchpin of the development team. This person is a coordinator of tasks, an architect, a mentor, and a developer at times. Individuals in this position typically have been through several assignments in other roles within the team, possibly all roles. Responsibilities include:

- taking leadership of the team from a management and mentorship standpoint. This role is crucial, as mentorship can make or break the team's productivity.

- analyze and set technical architecture requirements

- formulate potential classes, analyzing behaviors and interrelationships

- produce a high level technical summary

- assist in production of the documentation in consultation with the BAPC

Alliances are straightforward. The development team and the Object System Center backwall is be the ODPC 's alliance structure. Contact with the business area is more limited than for the BAPC who is in constant contact with the business area and is acting as a filter for the ODPC and the team.

Background: This individual should have served on several projects in the other roles and is expected to have demonstrated excellent command of the object design methods in use. The ODPC is also to have strong programming and analytic skills, good business knowledge, and strong project management training.

Class designer (CD)   The CD is to coordinate with the two coaches and produce a working document that forms a basis for defining the actual classes and their behaviors. These class structures are formulated around the analysis document, and the final result is a workable, programmable hierarchy. Other responsibilities include:

- design methods that fit the defined behaviors as created by the BAPC and the ODPC

- choose appropriate algorithms that are used to implement the behavior

- define the classes directly and define instance variables within classes

- define class protocols in a consistent and reliable manner

- code the classes in the language of choice in conjunction with the class constructors. This is to help keep the design and the code consistent.

The CD needs to maintain good contact and provide timely feedback to the ODPC and BAPC. Their analysis documents were what the CD used in the first place to design the hierarchy. The CD is primarily responsible for monitoring and ensuring that the class constructors remain on track and focus only on assigned work. A critical skill is to maintain an understanding of the business rules so that the class design matches the business requirements, stated or otherwise.

Background: Very strong object design skills, perhaps the strongest of the entire group. Strong programming skills in object languages. Good business skills are important to maintain good design.

Application integrator (AI) The AI performs the build tasks at regular intervals, but especially when a project is nearing completion—*packaging the final production version*. As such, the AI has several very important responsibilities:

- integrate changes as they are versioned by developers and verify the horizontal and vertical integrity within the system

- package versions for testing by using a machine dedicated to this task, which holds only the versioned code with no open edition or scratch code

- keep detailed records of failures and report to the appropriate developer. The AI often finds inconsistencies in the system and maintains a log. This often serves as a secondary tasklist for the development team when they have lulls in work load intensity.

- create detailed technical documentation and design documentation on the system

The AI is heavily reliant on the rest of the development team. Most of the AI's impact comes from this interaction. The AI produces defect reports that are distributed to the development team for correction. This interaction is to assure that all along the way, all members know which problems they are responsible for.

Background: Excellent group skills are a must in this position. Good project management skills can be helpful in maintaining the defect report list and following its progress through integration. Some programming skills are important, but testing and testing methodology skills are even more important. Version control system knowledge is important.

Class constructors (CC)   CCs implement the designs. Using the technical specifications and the CD's design templates and documentation, the individual classes are coded in conjunction with the CD who may also develop code. Each class created is to be individually tested and versioned prior to handing it off to the AI who then places it into a package at some regular interval. Responsibilities include:

- code the classes using the CD's defined algorithms and methods

- develop methods that assist in unit testing the classes and then test the classes

- document the structure of the class and comment the code (*very* important for the reuse engineers' later assessment of their value)

In-depth interaction with the CD assures that what is coded is what is designed. This is the main alliance for the CC with a similar alliance to the player/coaches of both types.

Background: Complete language training from introductory to advanced in the language of choice. Working knowledge of version control systems is a must (ENVY/Developer, etc.).

Systems area trainee (SAT)   System trainees are those people to whom the technology transfer is primarily effected. As part of the development team, they are the ones who are most likely to be the least experienced, from an object technology standpoint. After attending training classes in the programming language chosen, they assist as class constructors or as application integrators. Their primary function is to write code and to help develop the system test plan. Responsibilities include:

- code classes according to the design spec

- unit and system test, documenting the test process

- produce test cases/scenarios and test data while analyzing event flows for consistently correct behavior

SATs are individuals from the same business group as the BAPC and probably know, or report directly to, the BAPC in the business customer area. At the outset, there should be an alliance with the BAPC who can serve as a business perspective mentor. Coverage of the system during testing is crucial, and the BAPC is expected to assist the SATs by helping them map business event flows so that superior test cases can be generated.

Background: A SAT should be business oriented, but with technical programming ability. This ability does not have to be superior. Mentorship is provided for those SATs wishing to learn the development environment for a later rotation as a class designer.

Object system center facilities

As we undertook object projects and developed an understanding of the value inherent in assigning the roles and responsibilities defined above, we continued to develop in a geographically distributed manner. While the roles seemed appropriate, it became apparent that the leverage expected from the backwall team could only be fully realized by co-locating the development projects for the first three months of their life span. We often referred to this facility as the *object incubator* and proposed the model shown in Figure 4.4. In June 1993, we acquired the floor space and partitioned the

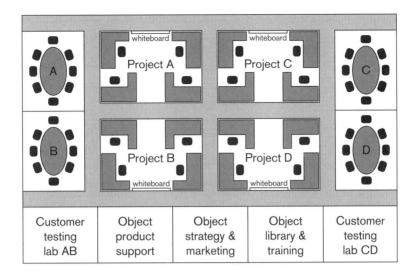

Figure 4.4   The OSC facilities plan

area to be similar to what is seen in the figure. However, after the change in corporate control and the cost cutting that ensued, we yielded the space and suspended the facilities plan.

OOPSLA '93 list of object technology center activities

In the OOPSLA '93 Workshop devoted to discussions about corporate object technology centers, we identified a multitude of functions provided by the many object technology centers represented. Table 4.2 lists these activities and their relative importance to the OSC. Table 4.3 provides a cross reference of that list of functions to the roles established in The Travelers' Object Technology Center. These functions are not the abstract responsibility of "The Center," but of the individuals serving in those roles.

The entries in the table are defined as follows:

- P—a primary OOTC activity

- S—a secondary OOTC activity

- N—not an OOTC activity

Table 4.2 Comparison of Object Systems Center activities and OOPSLA list

OOPSLA-defined OTC activities	OOTC focus
Education/knowledge broker	S
Build book library	S
Newsletters	N
Seminars	P
Mentoring	P
Support pilot projects	P
Apprenticeships	P
Object-oriented hot line	N
Customizing technology for projects	S
Monitoring project status	S
Drive cross-project information	P
Infrastructure for cross-project use	S
Change organizational culture	P
Reuse management	S
Manage vendor relationships	S
Coordinate training	N
Tool acquisition and licensing	S
Tool evaluation	S
Ensure unified view from consultants	S
Business strategy synchronization	P
Evaluate class libraries	N
Justify object technology center	N
Build common view of architecture	S
Contribute to state-of-the-art	S
Develop custom methods	S
Develop reusable frameworks	S
Develop handbooks	S
Coding guidelines	S

Table 4.2   Comparison of Object Systems Center activities and OOPSLA list (continued)

OOPSLA-defined OTC activities	OOTC focus
Reuse guidelines	S
Management presentations	N
Promote company activities externally	N
Lobby for support of technology	N

Table 4.3   Functions mapped to the backwall staff

Object System Center role	Assigned functions
Director of strategic object systems development	• networking, vision of architecture • technology transfer • pilot projects • coordination of efforts, communication • drive information across projects • build infrastructure for cross-organization use • change the culture & values of the organization • negotiate licensing agreements • business strategy synchronization • promotion of company activities outside • lobbying for appropriate support
Object evangelist and historian	• education/knowledge broker • newsletters and seminars • speaker on topics of interest • OO hot line • evaluate appropriateness of projects • ensure consultants and vendors remain consistent • promotion, selling, and PR • presentations to management for OT
Object projects controller	• getting a pulse on project status
Reuse engineer (Smalltalk, C++)	• customizing technology to organization • asset management • develop reusable frameworks • standards, guidelines for coding and reuse

Table 4.3 Functions mapped to the backwall staff (continued)

Object methods, standards & quality promotor	• education/knowledge broker • book library • training, how-to, coordination • customize methodology • general standards and guidelines • production of handbooks • design review guidelines
Vendor products and services researcher	• education/knowledge services contact • technology support/services/adaptation • OO hot line • customizing technology to organization • manage external vendor relationships • tools research, evaluation and acquisition
Object development player/coach	• technology transfer • mentoring, apprenticeships

Evolution

Pre-OSC *object development*

Prior to the establishment of the OSC, The Travelers' object technology projects were managed independently and generally did not leverage or share their common experiences and delivery products. What little sharing did occur was incidental and was almost always the result of informal discussions between members of the projects who had previously worked together.

Suspension of the OSC

As a result of the change in control in January 1994, the Object System Center initiative was suspended for one year. The stated motivation was to focus more efforts on controlling and cutting costs in the information systems areas in aggregate. In essence, senior management decided to mortgage the ability to leverage object development efforts, with the expectation of carrying on as scheduled in January 1995. In the meantime, we have returned to an operating mode where each business unit is proceeding with their object development efforts individually. However, as a result of the efforts undertaken in the two previous years, there is appreciation among the teams for the need to coordinate. Therefore, the OSC exists informally and in spirit, if not formally and physically.

Reinvigoration plan

The central aspect of this plan is to recapture the people that have been parceled out to the lines of business that are now building systems.

Lessons learned

Our past experiences have certainly taught us some valuable lessons. Many of them are repetitions of what is generally communicated in the popular literature about the trials and tribulations of those adopting object technology.

- educate management
- recruit a high-level sponsor
- set expectations appropriately
- learn from experienced peers
- recruit and carefully manage outside experts
- target developers based on personal motivation
- work in small, geographically close teams
- plan for new roles and skills

- target object-based applications judiciously

- invest in training

- recognize that analysis and design are difficult

- choose an object-oriented language carefully (hint: Smalltalk)

- evolve prototypes into production systems

- conduct regular design and code reviews

- focus on early performance

- position reuse as a long-term benefit

- develop organizational structures to promote reuse

- create reuse incentives

- develop object-oriented metrics

Below, in more detail, are what I believe are the three most important lessons we have learned.

People are everything

The quality and enthusiasm of the people in the organization is perhaps the single most influential element in achieving success in adopting and advocating object technology in a large organization. We seek two basic factors in evaluating whether the candidates are appropriate for this initiative. First, we must determine if the candidate has the basic combination of skills that are required for the position. That is a combination of technical competency, interpersonal skills, and learning potential. These are difficult to measure, but are noticeable when absent. The second factor is the individual's attitude, or level of desire to achieve success by applying himself to maximize and enhance those basic skills, mentioned above, to make the vision a reality.

Obviously, those without the skills are of little value to the initiative. Those with the skills, but without the proper attitude, are likely to be underperformers that drag on others, either through inaction or by not accepting their share of the responsibility. The important thing to notice is that this issue is entirely independent of the underlying technology. However, it is an organizational issue of incontestable importance, since efforts to change the development culture are entirely formed by the confluence of personalities that the initiators bring to the process. Without the right mix of people, sharing a common vision and lending their strengths to the effort, the initiative will fail. *Your people make things happen, not the technology.*

Solve real business problems

Do not become a technology looking for a problem to solve. Almost certainly, you will misapply the technology. Always begin with a well-defined business problem and seek to determine whether the object technology that you support is truly a solution match to the problem at hand. Do not try to create a business problem to solve or apply object technology where a more traditional solution will be acceptable, unless it is the long term direction to migrate toward a full object technology replacement.

Our first Smalltalk system, the Premium Audit Processing system is an example of technology searching for a business problem to solve. While the resulting technological product was serviceable and accomplished the goals outlined, it wasn't really needed and was never fully supported. Our business area did not feel a compelling need to develop a system which would address critical needs in this area. It was only after we investigated the business process and found an "opportunity" to help that we had a problem to solve. However, it was not a problem that was high in priority for attention or resources. This really became a problem for system testing and rollout, since there were other minor crises of greater importance that required the attention of the area's limited resources.

Our successful projects, Litigation Management and Customer Service Call Tracking, have been for areas that had demanding business requirements and difficult schedules. In remaining focused on solving the acute business problem within the time frame provided, we were able to present ourselves as committed partners that positively contributed to the bottom line operations.

One way to fail to impress the business areas with the capabilities of the center is to overdesign and overbuild a system. Another is to solve a relatively unimportant problem for the business area. Then object technology will be seen as a high-cost, low-return solution. *Choose projects carefully, and be sure the business needs are the true motivators.*

Time is money

Time is money. Research and technological knowledge are wonderful things…in a university. We live in a rather merciless commercial environment that is concerned only with return on investment and meeting deadlines. The question is always, "Who can do this cheaper, better, faster?" As we have more experience in improving our skills and growing our class library, we are better in quality, faster to deliver, and less expensive than traditional methods. All this means that using object technology has a less negative impact on the bottom line than, say, COBOL. The business areas are willing to fund us to provide this value, but not to play with new technology. As long as we maintain a focus on applied usage of object technology—focusing on real problems—and help our business partners meet objectives, things will be fine. No one has time for promises—waiting costs money. Develop working solutions up front and then mine them for storage and later reuse in the OSC. *Do not try to design and build generically useful stuff up front in isolation. Prove your competence through actual project work first.*

Conclusions

Building an object technology center is not for the faint-of-heart. There is a great deal of resistance to change in organizations, especially when the change is introduced as a replacement for the status quo. However, if you intend to pursue this path in a large organization, there is no better time than the present. Finding the core group of people that will make the vision a reality should be the first priority. This must be followed by a campaign to gain absolute support from one of the organization's key direction setters who has true authority to (a) ensure that the effort always has access to the necessary resources, and (b) remove any roadblocks. Once the executive sponsor is on board, begin solving real business problems to gain credibility and respect. From that point, the leverage can occur, and the original core group can begin to construct an object technology center that represents their collective vision of how object technology should be done in your company.

Acknowledgments

I would like to acknowledge the unique and valuable contributions at different levels and in different forms from each of the following individuals who worked directly on the Travelers' Object System Center initiative: Joe Correira, John Zack, Ed Zakowicz, Sirkka Johnson, Harrison Davis, Dave Hersey, Peter Troost, Kim Harnois Downes, Jennifer Pellei Pietropaolo, Lisa Pearson, Marc D'Antonio, Carole Rycki, Joon Brown,

Bob Eagan, Larry Girardi, Jimmy Nguyen, Bruce Hyre, Brian Blair, Eric Johnson, Kevin Miller, Sean Hickman, and Christa Rakich. Also many thanks to those whose names were not mentioned above, but provided other valuable direction and input.

Special thanks to Steven Stiling and Ken Rachford for their confidence in my abilities and encouragement to strive for greater achievements.

Finally, and most importantly, I must note the tolerance, patience, and loving support of my wife Marina during my long absences during crunch times and travel.

chapter 5

WilTel Technology Center

Jamie Erbes

Background and introduction

WilTel is one of The Williams Companies, Inc., a $5 billion corporation with headquarters in Tulsa, Oklahoma, that provides pipeline transportation of natural gas and petroleum products and nationwide digital telecommunications. WilTel is a full-service telecommunications company that provides data, voice and video products and services nationwide. WilTel owns and operates a nationwide fiber-optic network, one of only four in the United States, with access to more than 30,000 system miles. WilTel was founded in 1985 with the idea of threading fiber-optic cable through old decommissioned pipeline for the purpose of leasing data facilities to other carriers and large companies.

WilTel now employs about 3,800 people and serves a market ranging from sales and service of PBX and voice mail equipment, to long distance services, to specialized public network services such as Frame Relay and ATM (Asynchronous Transfer Mode). With a history and expected future of rapid company growth and a need for fast time-to-market of high technology products, WilTel saw bottom-line benefits of using object-oriented technologies for systems development.

In 1989, WilTel determined that cell-switching technology would provide the foundation from which WilTel could offer new and unique business communication solutions. We embarked on a path that would put WilTel at the leading edge of data communications technology.

WilTel created a research and development center in The Woodlands, Texas. This engineering group was dedicated to developing an ATM cell-switching network platform in which WilTel could control development of network management functions, signaling, and call processing. To accomplish this objective on the network, we focused on software development. We brought together a team of object-oriented programmers to develop a wholly unique network management and control system. Our commitment was to develop a vendor-independent network architecture in which WilTel maintains control over networking intelligence through software.

We established a pure object-oriented environment designed for rapid application development and deployment (RADD). Using RADD, we expected new software prototypes to be quickly developed and modified, and software-defined objects to be used and reused to further enhance the rapid deployment of new applications. This strategy is providing WilTel with the most important strategic and competitive advantage: flexibility. We can quickly add new applications and capabilities.

As with any innovative idea which shows promise within a pilot project, WilTel became anxious to scale the technology to the Enterprise. In late 1992, we began an effort to migrate the technology from the R&D center into the mainstream IS department. The first pilot projects in this effort quickly pointed out that in order to successfully gain any of the marketed benefits of OO technology (maintainability, higher quality software, software reuse—leading to higher productivity, etc.) as we scaled, our organization would need to put an infrastructure in place to manage this technology transfer.

Selling the idea of an object technology center (OTC) was not as difficult as some might expect. Our management had seen firsthand some hints of the benefits that WilTel could gain with the proper application of OO technology. WilTel management understood that to create and deliver high technology products and services, the effectiveness of our IS department would be the key to WilTel's success in the telecommunications market. They were very interested in applying the OO techniques they had witnessed in our smaller R&D efforts to Enterprise-wide business applications to boost WilTel's time-to-market advantage.

Our real argument was to convince management that OO was not in and of itself a silver bullet. Sprinkling the magic dust of OO on projects would not yield the golden calf. We

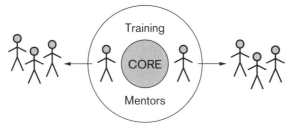

OST—leading the enterprise toward object technology
by providing training, mentorship, and code library
management for application development teams

Figure 5.1   Object technology center

believed that OO technology, combined with distributed
client/server architecture, sound software engineering practice, and proper library management, could yield the benefits WilTel desired. Without repeatable methodologies,
proper training, and visibility into an inventoried catalogue of
robust objects, our developers might produce a brown calf
with six legs (each designed and implemented differently),
two heads, and a tail that broke each time it flicked to the left.

To this end, we planned and implemented an object technology center (which we called the Object Services Team or
OST) in late 1993 (see Figure 5.1). Some of the immediate challenges before us included staffing and ongoing funding. Our
IS department is primarily a "charge back" environment,
obtaining the funding for projects from sponsoring business
units within the company. Creating software with reuse in
mind requires more time and effort. How would we convince
these projects that it was in the company's best interest to
increase the costs of their initial OO projects?

Our initial inclination was to create the OST as a support
team, just as necessary as other technical support teams such
as network and system administration groups. OST work
would not be billed back to individual business units initially.
OST costs would be rolled up and reflected in the IS per-hour

charge. This would leave the team unencumbered with spending time continually justifying and trying to split the cost of reusable objects amongst various projects. We found this direction to work best for our internal needs.

Another challenge before us was staffing and team building. There are many factors that differentiate a team from a group of individuals; we see the main difference being that the members of a team are all working towards common goals, while adhering to certain norms of conduct. The OST management realized that defining and publicizing these goals would have to be the first step in team building. We developed and published a business plan that served as the central tool for communicating our team's goals and objectives to all members of the Object Services Team as well as the rest of WilTel's organization.

To staff our newly defined team, we began a search internally and externally for highly qualified developers who possessed a wide range of skills. In order to succeed as a group of respected experts trusted to mentor the rest of the organization, the OST required top-notch development skills as well as diplomatic communication abilities. Internally, these individuals were also the most wanted and needed within the current application development teams and were often involved with existing development efforts. Line managers and supervisors were tasked to work together to identify personnel and individual transition plans. Support from executive management helped to validate the OST and encourage buy-in from line management.

Obtaining staff from outside the IS organization proved to be just as challenging. We looked toward consulting firms, contracting or head hunter agencies, as well as using recruitment techniques such as placing ads in regional newspapers and on the Internet. We looked for quality individuals having excellent communications skills and varied technical backgrounds. We hoped to find object-oriented experience levels ranging from entry-level to ten or more years of industry experience. Our recruitment search was difficult as corpora-tions began competing for the limited object-oriented exper-tise in the job market. We were never able to attract any individuals having 10+ years of object-oriented experience. We were mostly successful finding individuals having two to four years of experience.

Mission

The major objectives of the OST focused on developing and installing an information technology infrastructure that would facilitate the adoption of object-oriented, networked computing paradigms, as the standard architecture for the majority, if not all of the new software development projects. We expected that even though the infrastructure would evolve as we gained experience and as technology advanced, our goal was to have the baseline team solidly in place by the first quarter of 1994. The major activities and deliverables composing the infrastructure were:

System life cycle (SLC)   Continue to build and refine the methods/techniques, deliverables, and tools that should be used when developing or maintaining an object-oriented, Networked Computing application. This process will be itera-tive in nature and closely tied with the activities listed below.

Central object repository environment (CORE)   The cre-ation of a CORE is mandatory in order to effectively and effi-ciently manage objects and ensure their quality and re-usability. The CORE will need to handle objects developed in a variety of languages, store and associate diagrams and design documents as per the SLC, and allow for effective inquiry as to its contents.

Staff migration strategy   Develop a plan or strategy for migrating existing IS personnel associated with the tradi-tional method of application development to the new system life cycle. This will include a specific training regimen, pilot projects, and expected time frames to accomplish the baseline transition.

Object learning center (OLC)   The OLC will be an environment that contains the necessary staff, materials, and technology to learn and stay abreast of object technology and to provide technical training and education to the rest of the organization.

Technology research   This function will be responsible for staying abreast of new technology and advances in existing technology that have the potential for effectively addressing WilTel's business needs. Example areas of research include object-oriented operating systems (IBM/Apple: Pink, MicroSoft: Cairo) and continued progression of the object management group's CORBA standard and subsequent vendor implementation.

Activities

In order to accomplish the objectives and activities outlined above, it was important to put in place an organization and overall environment that facilitated communication and empowered the team to be successful. In building a strong software engineering basis we had to, as an organization, support some change in our culture. Edward Yourdon, author of *The Decline and Fall of the American Programmer,* summarizes his advice on how to build a quality software engineering organization:

- hire the best people you can

- pay special attention to proper training of your people

- provide an exemplary environment in which your people feel motivated to have fun and do good work

The most critical peopleware issue that organizations must address is that of hiring. We believe that quality people make quality organizations. We involved our staff in the interviewing process to get critical technical evaluations of candidates. We implored our human resources and executive management to alleviate some traditional salary constraints. If we expected to draw top talent, we had to be prepared to pay the commensurate salary. We also made an effort to sell Tulsa, Oklahoma. Tulsa is not generally associated with high-tech opportunities. We instead brought out the advantages that an easy-going life-style in the midwest offered.

The overriding concept that we wanted to foster in the OST was that of a team. We promoted an identity for the team, holding a contest amongst team members to select an official team logo for T-shirts and memo notes. Of the many factors that differentiate a team from a group of individuals, we saw the main difference being that the members of a team are all working towards a common goal(s), while adhering to certain norms of conduct. The business plan became the central tool for communicating our team's goals and objectives to all members of the OST; in fact, the team had heavy input into the contents of the document.

We also worked to create an environment or atmosphere that encouraged communication, innovation, education, and results. We adopted a number of activities along these lines; namely, a physically separate office space from the day-to-day business activities, an individually preferred dress code, flexible work hours, and weekly team lunches. Going forward, many of the infrastructure objectives and activities were directed towards creating our desired environment. Chief among these activities were the creation of the object learning center (OLC) and the technology research function; both of these tasks directly contributed towards innovation and education of the team. We also hoped to continue to focus on improving our physical office environment in areas such as an improved hardware lab, project team meeting rooms, appropriately sized offices, etc.

In addition to supporting the OLC, technology research functions and continued improvement in the physical office environment, we recognized that in order to develop in-house expertise on our stated technologies, we had to allow for and fund an aggressive and recurring tool acquisition and training program. This included placing high-power work stations and servers on the team members' desktops and labs, allowing for acquisition of new technology and software for both development support tools and production system use, and dedicating time and dollars to training and conferences. We recognized that given the technologies that we were deploying, increased tools and training were an integral factor, and in many cases a mandatory factor for success.

Good technical staff members are motivated by opportunities to learn new techniques and technologies. An organization that does not promote learning opportunities is leading its staff to obsolescence. One cannot expect loyalty from its underutilized and underchallenged staff. We wanted to emphasize that we expected quality work and would invest in adequate training to enable that quality work. With learning resources made available to the technical staff (in the form of libraries and organized skill-building sessions) we could improve the quality of our staff and make them feel their professional growth was a serious matter.

Evolution

Current status   With the creation of the Object Services Team in the IS organization, we began to lay the foundation necessary to effectively spread attainable benefits of OO development to the Enterprise. The Object Services Team provides support and expertise for all new platforms and development tools used in WilTel's software engineering and development efforts. With its creation, we proposed to put an infrastructure in place which would:

- develop, maintain, promote, and enforce a system life cycle

- develop and maintain a central object repository environment

- develop and maintain an object learning center

- provide technical programming support

- provide consultants on object-oriented projects

- develop and maintain reusable software components and tools

We implemented this infrastructure in the form of three distinct groups within the Object Services Team:

Central repository management (CRM) This group is responsible for managing the CORE, and performing testing and quality checks, and management over any object stored in the CORE. In managing the CORE, this group performs check-in/check-out/merge functions on the reusable objects contained within it, provides tools to peruse the CORE, and actively promotes the contents of the CORE. The first critical deliverable of this group was a functional system life cycle, which described the iterative process, deliverables, and project management check points.

Object technology research and learning center This group focuses its efforts in two basic areas: education and research. Activities in the education area include establishing and administering the Object Learning Center, conducting and coordinating object-related training, and promoting Wil-Tel's system life cycle.

The research portion is responsible for staying abreast of trends and new technology that may be applicable to WilTel's business problems. This task is accomplished by an ongoing review of industry literature, discussions with vendors and peer companies, and hands-on evaluations of new software, hardware, and networking technologies.

Mentorship and parts   This group focuses on providing object consultation to specific projects and to identify and (potentially) develop highly re-usable objects (i.e., Frameworks, Parts). As we roll out object development to other application teams across the enterprise, it is critical to provide a dedicated mentor who is SLC experienced (analysis, design, programming, and maintenance) and can act as a link with the Object Services Team functions (CORE, SLC).

Central repository management and total quality management

> **methodology** *n.*, a body of methods, rules and postulates employed by a discipline: a particular procedure or set of procedures—*Webster's Ninth New Collegiate Dictionary, 1988.*

Much has been said as to the selection and implementation of a methodology. A variety of definitions can be found to describe what a methodology involves. For clarification, the Object Services Team agreed on the following definitions:

- *Methodology*   a step-by-step plan for achieving some desired result. A software development methodology usually identifies the major activities—for example, analysis, design, coding, and testing—to be carried out, and indicates which people—users, managers technicians—should be involved in each activity and what roles they play.

- *Method*   a step-by-step technical approach for performing one or more of the major activities identified in an overall methodology. Thus, *object diagramming* is a method within the analysis and design phases of the Booch methodology.

- *System life cycle*   a complete process which goes beyond the activities of a development methodology to include activities specific to WilTel—for example, service request creation, AFE development, and change management

The central repository management (CRM) group has a focus on software engineering rather than code development. The CRM charter will be to develop, refine, publish, disseminate, and enforce a life cycle which is independent of a platform or development tools. Additionally, the group is also expected to manage and protect WilTel's corporate asset of collected objects.

Central object repository environment

The central object repository environment (CORE) is a collection area for objects, documentation, and other supporting files which are collectively used in several applications. Figure 5.2 gives a graphical depiction of the relationship of items included in the CORE.

The CORE is to provide structured object management independent of development platforms or languages. We expect the CORE to be implemented in such a way as to:

- segregate application specific objects from reusable objects

- provide powerful tools for browsing and investigating the library

- set and maintain procedures for access and update of objects

- allow for continuous review and refinement of reusable software components

- provide change/code management procedures which will allow a safe code migration from development, through quality assurance (QA) testing, to production implementation

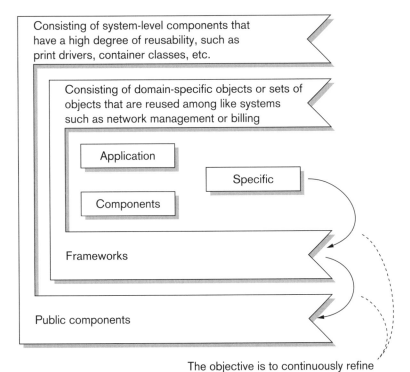

Consisting of system-level components that have a high degree of reusability, such as print drivers, container classes, etc.

Consisting of domain-specific objects or sets of objects that are reused among like systems such as network management or billing

Application

Specific

Components

Frameworks

Public components

The objective is to continuously refine software and migrate items from application-specific components to reusable components

Figure 5.2   Central object repository environment structure

Object technology research and learning center

Many current software engineering consultants point to adequate training as one absolute requirement of an organization which expects to take advantage of new technologies. We don't believe training to be the same thing as learning. We propose to use just-in-time (JIT) training practices to allow personnel to reinforce their formal training with on-the-job learning experience to immediately follow. Adequate training per person for software engineering topics is recommended to be 40–80 hours for analysis and design, and 30–100 hours for specific development tools. In order to cost-effectively provide this required level of training, we implemented in-house training capabilities through the Object Learning Center team. This team's charter includes:

- research and keeping abreast of software engineering advances and products

- use resources like Internet news groups, browsing, industry publications, conferences

- make knowledge accessible to other group members and developers by maintaining a library of resources

- establish and organize in-house training

- utilize and organize outside consultants when necessary

- maintain and create WilTel's own training classes and materials as needed

- provide access to new software evaluations

Mentorship and parts group

Consultants assigned to object-oriented projects are expected to provide mentoring services to application development teams. They are to be the communication links to the OST to keep both sides informed. We expected to dedicate at least one consultant to each project having less than seven members. For example, a project staffed with ten developers will require two dedicated mentors. In addition to consulting, team members are expected to identify, develop and maintain reusable software components in the corporate framework in the CORE. The framework will benefit from the team members using their consulting roles to gain input and direction for the framework. As keepers of the framework, their responsibilities are to insure that:

- reusable parts in new development efforts are identified

- existing parts are reworked and refined for reuse throughout the corporation

- parts are not abusively reused (fitting a square into a round hole)

- parts are not reinvented

- the SLC is known and enforced in the project teams

- project teams are informed of existing parts and help them properly reuse parts

- new tools are created which can be used internally (productivity tools)

The framework becomes the most important corporate asset. It will grow over the years according to WilTel needs. We want to use consultants as links to project teams to enable an interactive development of the framework and applications.

Table 5.1 summarizes the services provided by the WilTel Technology Center based on the list of possible activities of an object technology center developed at the workshop on Corporate Object Technology Centers at the 1993 Object-Oriented Programming, Systems, Languages, and Applications (OOPSLA) conference.

The entries in the table are defined as follows:

- P—a primary activity

- S—a Secondary Activity

- N—not an activity

Table 5.1 Comparison of technology center activities and OOPSLA list

OOPSLA-defined OTC activities	TC focus
Education/knowledge broker	P
Build book library	P
Newsletters	N
Seminars	S
Mentoring	P
Support pilot projects	P
Apprenticeships	S
Object-oriented hot line	P
Customizing technology for projects	S
Monitoring project status	N
Drive cross-project information	S
Infrastructure for cross-project use	P
Change organizational culture	P
Reuse management	P
Manage vendor relationships	N
Tool acquisition and licensing	S
Tool evaluation	P
Ensure unified view from consultants	S
Business strategy synchronization	S
Evaluate class libraries	P
Justify object technology center	N
Build common view of architecture	S
Contribute to state-of-the-art	P
Develop custom methods	P
Develop reusable frameworks	P
Develop handbooks	N
Coding guidelines	P
Reuse guidelines	P
Management presentations	S
Promote company activities externally	N
Lobby for support of technology	N

Lessons learned

Since the creation of the center, we have acknowledged some lessons learned and expect to learn more. Issues we have most noticed through our efforts are:

- be patient with the process of becoming the experts. Expertise is fostered through practice, and respect for expertise comes through repeatedly proving of value to the customer.

- insert the technology center into a management area of the organization where it is not at risk of being raided. For example, if the technology center is included within the management hierarchy of a group responsible for applications development, it becomes too convenient to borrow resources for that quick bug-fix, development effort, etc.

- just as with any other service-providing group, be careful to manage customer expectations well. Implement the group in defined stages, advertising all along that although a future item, such as a prescribed software life cycle, is within the team's scope, first or even second iterations shouldn't be taken as final material. Choose well-defined deliverables for the group that coincide with real business needs.

- the technology center addresses much more than just object technology. The issues surrounding the bringing of objects to the Enterprise brought out the fact that our IS organization was not positioned well to transition other new technologies into the Enterprise as well.

- executive management support is essential to the success of the center. This support is reflected in provision of human resources and systems resources as well as sending the message to the rest of the organization that the technology center is to be utilized as the center of expertise for software engineering.

Conclusions

Although WilTel's Technology Center is rather young, we have seen benefit in having an area of expertise to rely upon for advice and consulting in regard to new software engineering techniques and tools. We expect that as the Center grows and matures, it will earn the respect of the development staff by providing quality service. Moving forward, we have restructured the group so that the managerial reporting structure is closer to the executive level to minimize impact from day-to-day development projects. Additionally, we have opened up the scope of the center to embrace network and systems (hardware and operating systems) technologies. Whereas we were addressing more of the tactical issues surrounding object-oriented and client/server development, we will now strive to provide guidance along the entire scope of the development project. This can range from conceptual and feasibility studies working with the marketing product development group to defining implementation strategies with the development groups.

chapter 6

Survey of a cross-section of object technology centers

Introduction

This chapter presents a survey of several object technology centers, other than the four OTCs whose case studies are discussed in the previous chapters. The methodology used in the survey is as follows: Ten OTCs were contacted by telephone based on their participation at the First Conference on Object Technology Centers held in Stone Mountain, Georgia in 1995. Each representative was asked the same set of questions regarding his or her OTC.[*] This information was later emailed back for the purpose of verification and revision. Three organizations later decided not to contribute the information to this book. The rest of this chapter provides summary information about the following organizations: Andersen Consulting, Ascom Nexion, BellSouth, Microsoft, Northern Telecom, The Prudential Insurance Company of America, and Timberline Software.[†]

Andersen Consulting

Contributor of information: Manuel Cantoria

Name of the OTC or equivalent: Eagle Technology

Date when the center was started: 1991

Number of staff members: At start: 15   Now: over 100

Brief mission statement/goals statement: To define a new capability for software development based on a number of advanced concepts including distributed object computing, Integrated Performance Support™, advanced

---

[*] Respondents have provided information on their own OTCs that may or may not represent the corporation as a whole.
[†] In certain cases, the information provided was edited to conform to a common format and level of detail.

usability, and tailorability, using a comprehensive approach to object-oriented development of reusable application components, including:

- complete, end-to-end process that ties object design to re-engineering

- scalable organization/team model

- application architecture, including a component model, a growing library of reusable components, business process control, and dialog control

- Smalltalk-based development framework that fosters reuse and productivity

- technical architecture supporting multi-tier distribution and persistence

- open integration to desktop applications, high performance servers

- legacy systems developed outside of the Smalltalk-based framework

Funding

Source: Blend of centralized and distributed[*]

Timing: Blend of up-front and charge-back

Scope: Many diverse projects[†]

---

[*] The source of funding was centralized at the start. The funding is moving toward distributed (based on projects supported).
[†] At the start, the scope was only a few projects.

Activities

(P = primary activity; S = secondary activity; N = non-activity)

Table 6.1 Andersen Consulting activities

Activity	Focus
Education/knowledge broker	S
Build book library	S
Newsletters	N
Seminars	S
Mentoring	P
Support pilot projects	P
Apprenticeships	P
Object-oriented hot line	N
Customizing technology for projects	P
Monitoring project status	S
Drive cross-project information	S
Infrastructure for cross-project use	P
Change organizational culture	P
Reuse management	P
Manage vendor relationships	P
Tool acquisition and licensing	P
Tool evaluation	P
Ensure unified view from consultants	S
Business strategy synchronization	P
Evaluate class libraries	P
Justify object technology center	P
Build common view of architecture	P
Contribute to state-of-the-art	P
Develop custom methods	P
Develop reusable frameworks	P
Develop handbooks	P
Coding guidelines	S
Reuse guidelines	S
Management presentations	P
Promote company activities externally	P
Lobby for support of technology	P

Ascom Nexion

Contributor of information: Bob Rose

Name of the OTC or equivalent: Object Engineering Group

Date when the center was started: 1993

Number of staff members: At start: 1   Now: 5

Brief mission statement/goals statement[*]:   To promote object technology and code reuse throughout the corporation.

Funding

Source: Centralized

Timing: Up front

Scope: Many diverse projects[†]

Activities

(P = primary activity; S = secondary activity; N = non-activity)

Table 6.2   Ascom Nexion activities

Activity	Focus
Education/knowledge broker	P
Build book library	S
Newsletters	N
Seminars	S
Mentoring	P
Support pilot projects	P
Apprenticeships	S

---

[*] Informal statement
[†] Currently two projects

Table 6.2   Ascom Nexion activities (continued)

Activity	Focus
Object-oriented hot line	S
Customizing technology for projects	P
Monitoring project status	P
Drive cross-project information	P
Infrastructure for cross-project use	P
Change organizational culture	S
Reuse management	S
Manage vendor relationships	S
Tool acquisition and licensing	S
Tool evaluation	S
Ensure unified view from consultants	S
Business strategy synchronization	S
Evaluate class libraries	P
Justify object technology center	P
Build common view of architecture	S
Contribute to state-of-the-art	P
Develop custom methods	P
Develop reusable frameworks	P
Develop handbooks	N
Coding guidelines	P
Reuse guidelines	S
Management presentations	P
Promote company activities externally	S
Lobby for support of technology	S

BellSouth

Contributor of information: Norman Bunn

Name of the OTC or equivalent:
   Object Technology Resource Center

Date when the center was started: 1994

Number of staff members: At start: 20   Now: about 20

Brief mission statement/goals statement: To enable 40% of the applications development to start using object technology before 1997.[*]

Funding

Source: Centralized

Timing: Up front

Scope: Many diverse projects

Activities

(P = primary activity; S = secondary activity; N = non-activity)

Table 6.3   BellSouth activities

Activity	Focus
Education/knowledge broker	P
Build book library	S
Newsletters	N
Seminars	S
Mentoring	P
Support pilot projects	P
Apprenticeships	P
Object-oriented hot line	S
Customizing technology for projects	S
Monitoring project status	P
Drive cross-project information	N
Infrastructure for cross-project use	P
Change organizational culture	P
Reuse management	P
Manage vendor relationships	P
Tool acquisition and licensing	P

[*] Informal statement

Table 6.3   BellSouth activities (continued)

Activity	Focus
Tool evaluation	P
Ensure unified view from consultants	P
Business strategy synchronization	S
Evaluate class libraries	P
Justify object technology center	P
Build common view of architecture	S
Contribute to state-of-the-art	S
Develop custom methods	S
Develop reusable frameworks	P
Develop handbooks	S
Coding guidelines	P
Reuse guidelines	P
Management presentations	S
Promote company activities externally	S
Lobby for support of technology	P

Microsoft

Contributor of information: J. Patrick Thompson

Name of the OTC or equivalent:
   Technical Services: Software Architecture

Date when the center was started: 1994

Number of staff members: At start: 3   Now: 4

Brief mission statement/goals statement: To introduce explicit architectures organized around object-oriented and component technologies.*

---

* Informal statement

Funding

Source: Centralized

Timing: Up front

Scope: Many diverse projects

Activities

(P = primary activity; S = secondary activity; N = non-activity)

Table 6.4 Microsoft activities

Activity	Focus
Education/knowledge broker	P
Build book library	S
Newsletters	S
Seminars	S
Mentoring	S
Support pilot projects	S
Apprenticeships	N
Object-oriented hot line	N
Customizing technology for projects	S
Monitoring project status	N
Drive cross-project information	S
Infrastructure for cross-project use	P
Change organizational culture	P
Reuse management	N
Manage vendor relationships	P
Tool acquisition and licensing	P
Tool evaluation	P
Ensure unified view from consultants	S
Business strategy synchronization	N
Evaluate class libraries	N
Justify object technology center	P
Build common view of architecture	P
Contribute to state-of-the-art	N

Table 6.4   Microsoft activities (continued)

Activity	Focus
Develop custom methods	S
Develop reusable frameworks	P
Develop handbooks	S
Coding guidelines	S
Reuse guidelines	S
Management presentations	P
Promote company activities externally	N
Lobby for support of technology	P

Northern Telecom

Contributor of information: Marykay Wells

Name of the OTC or equivalent: Nortel Object Center

Date when the center was started: 1994

Number of staff members: At start: 5   Now: 24

Brief mission statement/goals statement[*]**:**   To ensure customer awareness of the conditions needed to run a successful object-oriented project; to mentor the customer on the concepts and technology needed for the project; to train the customer in the life-cycle development process; to identify reusable components that will speed the development process; to provide access to expert resources and knowledge to address specific design and technical issues; to supply advanced, but not always the absolute, leading edge of technological capabilities; and to offer reasonably priced and accessible products and services.

---

[*] Governing principles

Funding

Source: Blend of centralized and distributed

Timing: Blend of up-front and charge-back

Scope: Many diverse projects

Activities

(P = primary activity; S = secondary activity; N = non-activity)

Table 6.5   Northern Telecom activities

Activity	Focus
Education/knowledge broker	P
Build book library	S
Newsletters	P
Seminars	P
Mentoring	P
Support pilot projects	P
Apprenticeships	S
Object-oriented hot line	S
Customizing technology for projects	S
Monitoring project status	P
Drive cross-project information	P
Infrastructure for cross-project use	P
Change organizational culture	P
Reuse management	P
Manage vendor relationships	S
Tool acquisition and licensing	P
Tool evaluation	S
Ensure unified view from consultants	P
Business strategy synchronization	P
Evaluate class libraries	S
Justify object technology center	P
Build common view of architecture	P
Contribute to state-of-the-art	S

Table 6.5   Northern Telecom activities (continued)

Activity	Focus
Develop custom methods	P
Develop reusable frameworks	P
Develop handbooks	P
Coding guidelines	P
Reuse guidelines	P
Management presentations	P
Promote company activities externally	S
Lobby for support of technology	P

The Prudential Insurance Company of America

Contributors of information: Bill Reynolds, Xin Shu

Name of the OTC or equivalent: Object Technology Center[*]

Date when the center was started: 1994

Number of staff members: At start: 5   Now: 10

Brief mission statement/goals statement[†]:   To develop OO architectures for applications; to choose, customize, or develop OO methodologies for use in the company; and to provide guidance on the integration of legacy systems in the OO technology.

Funding

Source: Distributed

Timing: Charge back

Scope: Focus on an area, but larger scope

---

[*] Not a formal OTC
[†] Informal statement

Activities

(P = primary activity; S = secondary activity; N = non-activity)

Table 6.6   The Prudential activities

Activity	Focus
Education/knowledge broker	S
Build book library	S
Newsletters	S
Seminars	S
Mentoring	S
Support pilot projects	P
Apprenticeships	P
Object-oriented hot line	N
Customizing technology for projects	P
Monitoring project status	S
Drive cross-project information	P
Infrastructure for cross-project use	P
Change organizational culture	P
Reuse management	P
Manage vendor relationships	S
Tool acquisition and licensing	S
Tool evaluation	P
Ensure unified view from consultants	S
Business strategy synchronization	S
Evaluate class libraries	P
Justify object technology center	P
Build common view of architecture	P
Contribute to state-of-the-art	S
Develop custom methods	S
Develop reusable frameworks	P
Develop handbooks	P
Coding guidelines	P
Reuse guidelines	P
Management presentations	P
Promote company activities externally	P
Lobby for support of technology	P

Timberline Software

Contributor of information: Dan Corpron

Name of the OTC or equivalent: R & D Standards Group

Date when the center was started: Started in 1978 as a code reuse group; started using object-oriented techniques in 1993

Number of staff members: At start: 4   Now: 6

Brief mission statement/goals statement*:   To develop components for applications, and to educate developers in object-oriented technology.

Funding

Source: Distributed

Timing: Charge back

Scope: Many diverse projects

Activities

(P = primary activity; S = secondary activity; N = non-activity)

Table 6.7   Timberline Software activities

Activity	Focus
Education/knowledge broker	S
Build book library	S
Newsletters	N
Seminars	S
Mentoring	S
Support pilot projects	S

* Informal statement

Table 6.7   Timberline Software activities (continued)

Activity	Focus
Apprenticeships	S
Object-oriented hot line	N
Customizing technology for projects	P
Monitoring project status	N
Drive cross-project information	S
Infrastructure for cross-project use	P
Change organizational culture	P
Reuse management	P
Manage vendor relationships	P
Tool acquisition and licensing	P
Tool evaluation	P
Ensure unified view from consultants	S
Business strategy synchronization	P
Evaluate class libraries	P
Justify object technology center	P
Build common view of architecture	S
Contribute to state-of-the-art	S
Develop custom methods	S
Develop reusable frameworks	P
Develop handbooks	S
Coding guidelines	S
Reuse guidelines	S
Management presentations	S
Promote company activities externally	S
Lobby for support of technology	P

chapter 7

A comparative analysis of object technology centers

The structure of this chapter closely parallels that of Chapter 1. Chapter 1 is organized as a tutorial on the development of an OTC. The reader should refer back to Chapter 1 for specific advice and details on the covered topics. The focus of this chapter is to cross-reference and compare the OTCs described in Chapters 2–5 to the OTC framework described in Chapter 1 and to present some overall observations about OTCs that we have worked with over the years.

The goals of an object technology center

Due to the increasing rate of change in business, the culture surrounding software development must be extended from building systems that work to building business solutions that are adaptable to change. To this end many organizations are adopting OT.

Adopting OT is a fundamental organizational change that supports the creation of long-term, reusable, strategic solutions. However, without specific support for this change it will not occur.

The goal of an OTC is to be an effective change agent that:

- provides a model of the desired OT culture

- proactively seeks to change culture by bringing members of the corporate technical staff into personal contact with agents of change (e.g., consultants, mentors, educators)

- establishes policies, procedures, standards, and processes that support the desired culture

The desired end result is the institutionalization of the structures, processes, and outcomes that enable long-term success with OT. Thus an OTC is a specialized type of technology transfer center.

In Chapter 1 we defined the technology transfer goals of an OTC as:

G1 drive acceptance of object technology

G2 ensure success of projects using object technology

G3 transfer expertise to development staff

G4 mature the OO process being used by the corporation

G5 define effective roles of persons working on OO projects

G6 assist with the selection of the appropriate pilot OO projects

The following four tables relate each of the case studies from Chapters 2–5 to the goals outlined in Chapter 1. In the first column, we have listed related activities as described by each of the contributing corporations. The next six columns cross-reference that activity to the corresponding generic goals.

This table should not be interpreted as a definitive guide to the goals of the listed OTCs. It only lists those goals the authors chose to describe in their contributed chapter.

Table 7.1   Case studies: relationship to generic goals—IBM

IBM OTC specific goals	G1	G2	G3	G4	G5	G6
Expand and improve the OOTC document library to cover important aspects of object technology and the object-oriented development process		X	X	X		
Provide high-quality mentoring support throughout the development process		X	X		X	X
Understand, and help find solutions for, IBM's object-oriented education needs		X	X			
Increase penetration of OOTC information and other object technology within the labs	X					
Help development sites create object-oriented support organization		X	X	X		
Promote increased understanding of IBM's object-oriented products and strategies	X					

Table 7.2 Case studies: relationship to generic goals—BNR

BNR OTC specific goals	G1	G2	G3	G4	G5	G6
Develop handbooks for design and processes, methodologies, and notations				X	X	X
Develop handbooks for management progress metrics, milestone planning, design complexity metrics		X	X	X		
Provide technical consulting on domain analysis and design		X	X	X		
Provide management consulting to managers of object-oriented projects	X	X			X	X
Fund research into high-risk areas		X				
Coordinate tool evaluation and development efforts		X	X			
Provide list of consultants-for-hire to managers		X				X
Provide technology and management training	X	X	X			

Table 7.3 Case studies: relationship to generic goals—The Travelers

Travelers OTC specific goals	G1	G2	G3	G4	G5	G6
Leverage the total corporate investment in object technology	X	X				
Expedite knowledge transfer across the organization	X	X	X	X		
Facilitate corporate-wide design and code reuse to reduce development costs and cycle times, while improving overall quality		X	X		X	

Table 7.4 Case studies: relationship to generic goals—WilTel

WilTel OTC specific goals	G1	G2	G3	G4	G5	G6
Build and refine methods/techniques, deliverables, and tools that should be used when developing or maintaining an object-oriented, networked computing application		X	X	X		X
Create a central object repository environment to effectively and efficiently manage and ensure its quality and reusability		X				X
Develop a plan/strategy for migrating existing IS personnel to the new system life cycle		X			X	

Table 7.4   Case studies: relationship to generic goals—WilTel (Continued)

WilTel OTC specific goals	G1	G2	G3	G4	G5	G6
Develop object learning center that will create an environment that contains the necessary staff, materials, and technology to learn and stay abreast of object technology and to provide technical training and education to the rest of the organization	X	X	X	X		
Stay abreast of new technology and advances in existing technology that have the potential for effectively addressing the organization's business needs		X		X		

OTC interactions

The case studies do not specifically address the issue of OTC interactions, so we will make some brief observations based on our independent knowledge of these OTCs. When the BNR OTC was set up, careful attention was given to the organizational placement of the OTC. One of the authors was a consultant to BNR and assisted in the establishment of the BNR OTC. During that period, the author accompanied OTC personnel on visits to the heads of other peer groups. We visited many groups including the process group, testing group, tool development group, and the reuse group. Attention to these interactions has markedly contributed to the success of the BNR OTC.

Conversely, we have seen many OTCs reorganized out of existence due to lack of attention to these interactions. Less serious, but still insightful to note, is an incident involving representation on a panel at a well known international OO conference. One of the authors was invited to be a panelist along with an employee of one of the companies represented in this book. The employee is not a member of the OTC, but works for another center within the company in question. When news of the composition of this panel reached the members of the OTC, the comments made by the OTC staff and management revealed an underlying tension with the other corporate center. We believe that tension such as this should not be left unresolved.

Setting up an OTC

As far as we know, all of the OTCs were formed because of bottom-up pressure to do so. Thus, in each case, the proponents had to argue the business case for the establishment of their OTC. There are two fundamental arguments we have seen:

- existence
- cost reduction and avoidance

We elaborate on these arguments in the business justification section below.

Funding models

Table 7.5 refers to Figure 1.10.

Table 7.5   Funding models

	IBM	BNR	Travelers	WilTel
Funding source				
centralized		X		
distributed	X		X	X
blend				
Funding timing				
up-front	X	X		X
charge-back				
blend			X	

Table 7.5   Funding models (Continued)

	IBM	BNR	Travelers	WilTel
Funding scope				
many diverse projects	X		X	X
single family of projects		X		
focus on an area, but larger scope included				

Business justification

The funding models are related to the business justification.

The existence argument focuses on the idea that in order for object technology to succeed at the corporate level, an OTC is required. This was the essence of the BNR argument. Centralized, up-front funding is consistent with this type of business justification.

The cost reduction argument (internal mentors are cheaper than external consultants) was a much stronger factor in the IBM case. Distributed, charge-back funding is consistent with this type of business justification.

Organizational structure and staffing

We have worked with a large formal OTC with a staff of over 30. We have also worked with one-person OTCs with no formal organization charter. We believe that both types of organizations can benefit from the information in this book. Table 7.6 indicates the type of staff roles included in each of the case studies:

Table 7.6   Staff roles

Staff category	IBM	BNR	Travelers	WilTel
Board of directors		X		
Director	X	X	X	X

Table 7.6   Staff roles   (Continued)

Staff category	IBM	BNR	Travelers	WilTel
Mentors	X		X	X
Reuse staff			X	X
Process staff	X	X	X	X
Quality assurance staff		X	X	X
Training coordinator		X		X
Coordinator for tool acquisition and vendor relationships		X	X	X

Activities

In this section we group the activities listed in the matrix developed at an OTC workshop into the categories described in Chapter 1.

Shielding projects from corporate politics

The observed activities in this category are:

- convince management that OO technology is viable

- get process waivers

- fight the "iterative process" versus "waterfall" funding battle

- get metrics waivers so the OO projects are not evaluated on LOC measures

- lobby for support for investment in training, mentoring, tools, etc.

The closest matching activities from the OTC matrix are listed in Table 7.7:

CHAPTER 7:   A COMPARATIVE ANALYSIS

Table 7.7
(P = primary activity; S = secondary activity; N = non-activity)

Supporting activities—politics	IBM	BNR	Travelers	WilTel
Management presentations	P	S	N	S
Lobby for support of technology	P	N	N	N
Justify object technology center	P	S	N	N
Business strategy synchronization	N	N	P	S

Mentoring and apprenticeships

All OTCs should include this category of activity in their portfolios. Notice that all of the OTCs, except BNR, rate at least three of the activities in this category as "primary." BNR rates none of them as primary. At one point this caused the BNR OTC to acquire the nickname of the "Process Center" as opposed to the OTC.

The closest matching activities from the OTC matrix are listed in the following table:

Table 7.8
(P = primary activity; S = secondary activity; N = non-activity)

Supporting activities—mentoring	IBM	BNR	Travelers	WilTel
Mentoring	P	S	P	P
Support pilot projects	P	S	P	P
Apprenticeships	P	N	P	S
Object-oriented hot line	P	S	N	P
Customizing technology for projects	P	N	S	S
Monitoring project status	S	N	S	N

Creating and distributing handbooks

Object technology must be formalized and customized to each organization. To this end, OTCs typically create handbooks in the following areas:

- process

- testing

- design guidelines

- metrics

- reuse

The closest matching activities from the OTC matrix are listed in the following table. All but The Travelers OTC rate the majority of these activities as "Primary." The Travelers rates none of them as "Primary." This is another example of the variety amongst OTCs.

Table 7.9
(P = primary activity; S = secondary activity; N = non-activity)

Supporting activities—handbooks	IBM	BNR	Travelers	WilTel
Develop handbooks	P	P	S	N
Develop custom methods	P	P	S	P
Coding guidelines	P	S	S	P
Reuse guidelines	P	P	S	P
Contribute to state-of-the-art	S	S	S	P

Supporting reuse

An analysis of the table below shows a marked difference between WilTel and the other three OTCs. All of the OTCs have some activities related to reuse, but only WilTel rates the majority of the reuse activities as "Primary."

Table 7.10
(P = primary activity; S = secondary activity; N = non-activity)

Supporting activities—reuse	IBM	BNR	Travelers	WilTel
Develop reusable frameworks	N	N	S	P
Evaluate class libraries	P	N	N	P

Table 7.10   (Continued)
(P = primary activity; S = secondary activity; N = non-activity)

Supporting activities—reuse	IBM	BNR	Travelers	WilTel
Reuse management	S	N	S	P
Infrastructure for cross-project use	S	S	S	P
Drive cross-project information	P	S	P	S
Build common view of architecture	N	N	S	S

Types of OTCs

As noted in Chapter 1, an analysis of the many OTCs we have worked with shows that they tend to cluster into two different types of OTCs:

- consulting groups

- infrastructure groups

Corporate consultants

OTCs in this category devote most of their staff positions to mentoring and training. Funding for this type of OTC tends to be based on the fact that employee consultants are much cheaper than external consultants. The IBM OTC is a prime example of this category of OTC.

Corporate infrastructure

OTCs in this category focus on reuse, process, and handbook creation. Some staff positions may be devoted to obtaining ISO certification for an OO process. The focus is on producing written material rather than giving verbal advice on specific problems. Funding is based on reducing duplicated effort, increasing quality, reducing risk, justifying existence. Without an OTC, there will be no infrastructure, and without an infra-structure OT will not succeed at the corporate level. Table 7.11 relates the case studies to the type of OTC.

Table 7.11
(P = primary activity; S = secondary activity; N = non-activity)

Type of OTC	IBM	BNR	Travelers	WilTel
Corporate consultants	P	N	P	S
Corporate infrastructure	S	P	S	P

Lessons learned

In Chapter 1 we listed the following lessons learned:

- strive for a formal repeatable process

- don't wait for a formal process before you let your experts mentor

- aim for a mixture of short term tangible results with longer term idealistic goals. An organization can't go from level 1 to level 5 in six months.

- avoid methodology wars—learn to think in terms of a meta-process

- mentor in pairs to minimize personality problems and improve continuity

- get the best people

- the best technical gurus may not make the best mentors

- pay close attention to corporate politics or you may wind up reorganized out of existence

- external audits will save you a lot of grief

- use your board of directors

However, the major lesson learned is that unless there is someone charged with analyzing your own corporate experience and taking actions based on this analysis, the lessons will not be learned perhaps until it is too late to prevent a major disaster. An OTC is an ideal organization for implementing a continuously improving OT culture.

Comsoft—the meta-OTC

As noted in chapter one, Comsoft serves as an OTC for OTCs. As such Comsoft:

- maintains an inter-OTC forum for the sharing of experiences

- publishes an OTC newsletter and coordinates OTC conferences and workshops

- monitors and coordinates the international research of interest to OTCs

- sorts through the research results, commercial hype, and products

- conducts the basic research needed to fill the gaps where knowledge is lacking

- synthesizes the "good stuff" into usable handbooks, tools, and recommendations

Further information is available via email at

info@comsoft.southern.edu

or on the Web at

http://www.comsoft.southern.edu

Summary and observations

In the final analysis, OT is about people and the way they think and work. It can only thrive within a supportive software development culture. It is the job of the OTC to create and institutionalize an OT culture.

Cultures are not limited to ethnic groups. Anywhere that one finds a group of individuals with a shared set of stories, rituals, legends, icons, heroes, accepted behaviors, and defined roles, you have a culture. Some groups take their culture very seriously, and actively try to manage and maintain their culture. The French, for example, spend more time trying to manage their culture than Americans. The same is true of corporations. For years, IBM was famous for its well defined culture; roles were well defined, employees didn't have to guess as to what behavior was acceptable—you just knew. There were established rituals and icons, and many well circulated legends. As a consultant to many different companies, one of the authors gets to observe numerous cultural icons, heroes, and legends related to object technology. One company has a Reuse Rabbi, in another the lead framework architect is known as the Chief Conehead.

Most companies realize that adopting OT represents a paradigm shift, but many fail to realize that sustaining a paradigm shift requires more than training, mentoring, and introducing new processes. Sustaining a paradigm shift requires a new culture. Written processes, company rules, new compilers, and CASE tools are needed to institutionalize a culture, but they do not constitute or create a culture. A new corporate culture is created only when its employees identify with a new set of stories, rituals, heroes, icons, etc.

Corporations tend to understand how to institutionalize a fledgling culture, but they often give little thought on how to manage the introduction of a new culture. Evidence of this can be seen by analyzing the activities that companies assign to their OTC. An analysis of the case studies in this book finds few activities specifically aimed at fostering the creation of a new set of stories, rituals, roles, icons, etc.

The creation of a culture used to be a grassroots event with oral stories and traditions handed down from generation to generation, but Madison Avenue and Hollywood have shown us that cultural icons and rituals can be created almost overnight. We are not suggesting that OTCs create legends, but rather that they deliberately foster their creation. For example, a corporation can set up a project for overwhelming, legend-type, success by careful choice of the system to be developed, and judicious assignment of personnel to the project. Obviously, not every project can have all the best staff with ample external mentoring support, but your first project should be a carefully engineered spectacular success. Add in some deliberate marketing of this success and voila, a legend.

The creation of a written process can help to institutionalize a culture, but the creation of new roles and career paths for employees helps to directly establish a culture. Roles related to an OT culture include project reuse coordinator, repository librarian, prototyper, modeler, pattern harvester, chief framework architect, and application assembler. The more clearly these roles are defined by an OTC, paired with job titles, and put on business cards, the better they help to establish the desired culture. If the roles happen to acquire a colorful title like Chief Conehead or Reuse Rabbi, so much the better. Latch onto those icons and foster them.

To become a part of the culture, a potential cultural artifact must be widely circulated. Multiple means should be employed for this. The OTC Web page, the OTC newsletter, email, project meeting announcements, hallway bulletin boards, inter-office mail, and word of mouth should all be used.

A sometimes forgotten part of managing the introduction of a new culture is managing the extinction of incompatible pieces of the old culture. Some of the old legends, icons, roles, and rituals must be abandoned. To achieve this, not only must policies and procedures relating to the old culture be changed, but the old cultural attitudes must also be extinguished. Cartoons seem especially suited to the task of pointing out the absurdity of certain cultural practices from the old paradigm. Often this happens spontaneously. As we wander the labyrinth of corridors between cubicles in corporation after corporation, we notice the popularity of pinning up mutated cartoons on cubical walls. Dilbert and the Far Side seem to be among the most popular. The mutations are created with a splash or two of white-out and the name of a particular project, process, or local ritual penned in place of the whited-out text. Why not have an editorial page in the OTC newsletter where the best of these are reprinted and elaborated on in the editorial text? A prize could be offered for submissions that get printed, and the collection could adorn a well-placed bulletin board next to the coffee pot.

Obviously, cartoons, colorful titles for roles, and legendary success stories do not form the core foundation for success with object technology. Solid technical skills in object-oriented analysis and design, proper management metrics and techniques for controlling iterative, incremental, software development, and a well-documented process with a strong quality-assurance component are required. But cultural factors are also important.

Most OTC activities will be focused on the technology itself and related policies, processes, and procedures. But a successful OTC will also address cultural factors. Culture is about people. When cultures change, employees may lose rituals and other aspects that are personally important to them. An OTC should interview employees to determine what they miss about the old culture and then devise ways to make sure that employees understand how they can attain these same values and benefits within the new culture. The OTC should provide an example of the new culture within its own staff, and should train its staff on paradigm shift issues as well as on technology issues. The OTC should insure that the OT training curriculum includes reference to the new cultural legends and icons, and that at least one of the instructors is a master story teller. In addition, an OTC could create awards and special recognition ceremonies for things like "best pattern of the month."

In summary, it is our contention that an OTC should address a wide range of issues. Most corporate software development practices are sorely out of synchronization with the business needs of the corporation. OT represents a chance to bring the software development practices and culture back into line with business needs. However, this will not happen without a comprehensive coordinated effort. There are several options open to a corporation as how to coordinate this effort. We have found that many companies are creating an OTC specifically for this task. In this book we have tried to address all the relevant factors for the creation and maintenance of a successful OTC, as well as share case studies from a number of existing OTCs. It is the authors' and publishers' sincere hope that this book will prove to be of practical help to you in assisting your company's adoption of OT.

About the authors

John Cunningham is currently a senior software engineer for Object Technology International where he is focusing on business component design and targeted consulting. He has recently moved to this position from the Travelers Insurance Companies where he was manager of object architectures. Previously he has been a consultant with Andersen Consulting and Computer Sciences Corporation. John can be reached at *75054.1406@compuserve.com*.

Jamie Erbes has led several object-oriented and advanced technology projects as senior manager at WilTel Network Services. Her success in this role led to her selection in *Open Computing's* "Top 100 Women in Computing" in 1994. Since her family's relocation to the west coast, she now telecommutes as an internet software architect for WilTel Internet Services. Jamie can be reached at *jamie.erbes@wiltel .net*.

Tom Guinane is a senior programmer in IBM's Object-Oriented Technology Center. He is co-founder of the organization and currently focuses on object-oriented education, metrics, management consulting, and project estimation. Tom's present address is *IBM Corporation, Room F104, 555 Bailey Avenue, San Jose, CA 95141*.

Geoff Hambrick is currently the technical lead of IBM's Software Group Technology Center. Prior to this he was one of the lead consultants in IBM's Object-Oriented Technology Center where he mentored first- time users of object technology on projects within IBM. Geoff's present address is *IBM Corporation, MS 9542, 11400 Burnet Road, Austin, TX 78759*. He can also be reached at *geoff@austin.ibm.com*.

Timothy Korson is a senior partner in Software Architects, and executive director of Comsoft, a non-profit consortium for OTCs. He is an organizer of the annual conference on object technology centers and the ongoing series of OOPSLA workshops for members of corporate object technology centers. He has authored articles on transitioning to object technology, is a columnist for *Object* magazine, and has given tutorials at numerous international conferences on how to establish an OTC. Dr. Korson has extensive experience applying object-oriented techniques to solve business problems, and in particular has helped numerous organizations establish and sustain an OTC. He can be reached at *korson@comsoft.southern.edu*.

Tom Kristek is the manager and co-founder of IBM's Object Oriented Technology Center. In addition to managing the day-to-day operations of the OOTC, he focuses on issues of effective technology deployment. Tom can be reached at *tom_kristek@vnet.ibm.com*.

Gerard Meszaros is currently an object technology consultant at Object Systems Group specializing in software architecture. He has recently moved to this position from Bell Northern Research (BNR), where he was the founder and chief architect of the Generic Services Framework (GSF) project. He was also the founder of the GSF Object Center and managed it during its first year of operation. Prior to the GSF project, Gerard had many years of experience designing telecommunications software and managing software development projects. He can be reached at *gerard@osgcorp.com*.

Vijay Vaishnavi is professor of computer information systems at Georgia State University and research director of Comsoft. He is an organizer of the annual object technology centers conference and an organizer of the series of OOPSLA workshops on the role of corporate object technology centers. Dr. Vaishnavi has published widely, authoring over 65 articles, and is the information technology editor for *DATA BASE*. He is currently directing a research group that develops handbooks that are of direct interest and benefit to object technology centers and conducts research to fill gaps in the knowledge areas of the handbooks such as object-oriented metrics and reuse. He can be reached at *vvaishna@gsu.edu*.

index

handbooks (continued)
    notations 91
    progress metrics 91
    test processes 91
Helm, Richard 108
heroes 188
high-level corporate commitment 105

I

IBM 36–38, 73, 177, 180, 181, 183–186, 188, 193, 194
icons 188, 189
information broker 93
infrastructure for cross-project use 20, 75, 92, 132, 156, 162, 164, 165, 167, 169, 171, 173, 185
infrastructure groups 185
integration methodology definition 98
interactions 9
international research 187
inter-office mail 189
inter-OTC forum 187
investment in
    mentoring 182
    tools 182
    training 182
IS personnel migration plan 178
ISO certification 185

J

Johnson, Ralph 108
justify object technology 20
justify object technology center 75, 92, 102, 132, 156, 162, 164, 166, 167, 169, 171, 173, 183

K

knowledge transfer 178
Korson, Tim 34, 86, 87, 194
Kristek, Tom 35, 194

L

legends 188, 189
lessons learned 105
life-cycle funding battle 182
lobbying for support of technology 21, 76, 92, 133, 156, 162, 164, 166, 168, 170, 171, 173, 183

M

manage vendor relationships 20, 75, 92, 132, 156, 162, 164, 165, 167, 169, 171, 173
management presentations 21, 76, 92, 102, 133, 156, 162, 164, 166, 168, 170, 171, 173, 183
management training 91, 178
managing consultants 95
managing objects 146
mandate 86, 91, 107
mandate evolution 103
McGregor, John 34
mentoring 20, 22, 23, 50–62, 75, 92, 94, 132, 151, 154, 156, 162, 163, 165, 167, 169, 171, 172, 176, 183, 186, 189
mentoring support 177
Meszaros, Gerard 83, 194
meta-process 186
methodology 146, 151
methods 178
metrics 26
Microsoft 160, 166–168
mission 91
modeler 189
monitoring project status 20, 75, 92, 132, 156, 162, 164, 165, 167, 169, 171, 173, 183

N

new technology 179
newsletters 20, 28, 75, 92, 93, 132, 156, 162, 163, 165, 167, 169, 171, 172

Nortel Object Center 168
Northern Telecom (NT) 84, 160, 168, 169, 170

O

object center evolution 103
object diagramming 151
Object Engineering Group 163
object incubator 130
object learning center 179
Object-Oriented Technology Center (OOTC) 36, 39–81
object repository 146, 150, 152, 153
Object Systems Center (OSC) 111–119, 121, 134, 139
object technology center (OTC) 2, 170
Object Technology Centers Conference 160
Object Technology Resource Center 164
object-oriented education 177
object-oriented hot line 20, 75, 92, 132, 156, 162, 164, 165, 167, 169, 171, 173, 183
object-oriented products and strategies 177
object-oriented support organization 177
OMTool 96
OO process 177, 185
OO technology 36, 37, 182
OOTC document library 177
OOTC information 177
organization and staffing 86
organizational structure 181
OT culture 176, 188
OT match-maker 73
OTC interactions 179
OTC newsletter 187, 189, 190
OTC types 185, 186
OTC Web 189
outcomes 176

P

pattern harvester 189
people-ware issues 148, 149
personality problems 186
pilot OO projects 177
policies 176
politics 183
procedures 176
process handbooks 99
process ownership evolution 103
processes 176
products 187
project management processes definition 99
project meeting announcements 189
project reuse coordinator 189
promote company activities externally 21, 76, 92, 103, 133, 156, 162, 164, 166, 168, 170, 171, 173
prototyper 189
Prudential Insurance Company of America 160, 170, 171

R

R & D Standards Group 172
rapid application development and deployment (RADD) 143
recommendations 187
repository librarian 189
requests for framework support (RFS) 97, 98, 101
requirements capture methodology 97
requirements modelling methodology 97
research 91, 147, 178
research results 187
reuse 27, 107, 184
    guidelines 21, 76, 92, 101, 133, 156, 162, 164, 166, 168, 170, 171, 173, 184
    management 20, 75, 92, 132, 156, 162, 164, 165, 167, 169, 171, 173, 185

Reuse Rabbi 188, 189
Reuse Technology Support Center 38
Reynolds, Bill 170
rituals 188, 189
roles 189
Rose, Bob 163

S

seminars 20, 75, 92, 93, 132, 156, 162,
    163, 165, 167, 169, 171, 172
setting up an OTC 180
shielding projects from corporate
    politics 182
Shu, Xin 170
sizing effort 105
software agreements (SA) 100
Software Architects 86
Software Development Education
    Council 36
staffing 15, 41–44, 89, 145–147, 181
standards 176
stories 188, 189
structure evolution 104
structures 176
success of projects 177
support pilot projects 20, 75, 92, 132,
    156, 162, 163, 165, 167, 169,
    171, 172, 183
System Software Development
    Tools 38

T

Technical Services
    Software Architecture 166
techniques 178
technology training 91, 178
technology transfer center 176
test methodology definition 98
The OOTC Workbook-Driven Ap-
    proach 64, 77–79

Thompson, J. Patrick 166
Timberline Software 160, 172, 173
tool acquisition and licensing 20, 75,
    92, 132, 156, 162, 164, 165,
    167, 169, 171, 173
tool development 91
tool evaluation 20, 75, 91, 92, 132,
    156, 162, 164, 166, 167, 169,
    171, 173
tools 178, 187
    acquisition 96
    development 178
    evaluation 96, 178
training 147, 153
training programs 93
transcribe-and-converge technique 59
Travelers, The 110–113, 120–122, 124,
    131, 134, 139, 178, 180, 181,
    183, 184, 186, 193

V

Vaishnavi, Vijay 34, 194
Vlissides, John 108

W

waivers
    metrics 182
    process 182
Wells, Marykay 168
why object technology? 85
WilTel 142–145, 147, 149–152, 154,
    155, 158, 178–181, 183, 184,
    186, 193
word of mouth 189
written process 189

Y

Yourdon, Edward 147